50 MoMents

SCRAPBOOK THE PAGES THAT
Matter Most

by
Lisa bearnson

creating **Keepsakes**

INTRODUCTION

My mom and dad inspire me in so many ways—and recently they inspired me to create a special kind of scrapbook.

My parents compiled a scrapbook that's full of their best advice and wisdom, and the honest-to-good-ness truth according to them. It's a scrapbook I'll love and cherish all my days; I know it will offer me advice and comfort even after my parents are gone.

That scrapbook is the truth of who my parents are; it's filled with their love, their hopes, their dreams.

And that's got to be one of the most important reasons to scrapbook.

To share ourselves with pictures and words.

To celebrate our successes, to show what we've learned from our mistakes.

To remember who we are, to set goals for our lives, to share how we care for others.

In this book, you'll find the 50 moments that I think are most important to scrapbook, the scrapbook page topics that matter the most.

I hope this book will be a starting place for you to tell the stories that are most important to you, to share the values that define who you are, to make the pages that really matter most.

Lisa Bearnson

contents
THE MOMENTS

21. Think Big, Dream Big!

22. Always Keep Learning

23. Your Best Is Good Enough

24. Experience

25. Family

26. I'm Sorry

27. Friendship

28. Pay It Forward

29. Think Big

30. Thank You, Thank You, Thank You

31. On Schedule

32. Be Happy

33. Take Care

34. It's the Truth

35. Be Kind

36. Write How You Feel

37. I Love You

38. It's a Mistake

39. Enjoy Life

40. Be Patient

41. Respect

42. Shhh—It's a Secret!

43. Silence Is Nourishing

44. Keep It Simple

45. Treasure Chest

46. Working for a Living

47. Family Traditions

48. A Few of My Favorite Things

49. Just Say Yes!

50. I Love Home

#1 TALENTS AND GIFTS

Why: To share your strengths, to pass along your legacy.

What are your talents and gifts? When did you discover your talents? How have others' talents enriched your life?

I've been an entrepreneur since the time I was very young. As a child, I dragged a Hoover around the neighborhood and vacuumed floors. I sold frozen berries, zucchini squash and Christmas cards door to door and of course set up lemonade stands on my front porch. I remember one particular summer afternoon. Nadine Kitchen and I had made the best darn batch of lemonade. Adults in cars and kids on bikes whizzed by without stopping. After a couple of hours, we were feeling a little deflated. During this time, my older sister, Debbie, came home and immediately bought a glass telling us how great it was. She went in the house, and then several minutes later came out to buy another glass insisting she was dying of thirst. She did this several more times until I think she spent around $5.00 of her money (that's a lot of lemonade!).

Debbie's example of true kindness and compassion are still with me today. We have a rule that our family always buys from a child—even if we're in a hurry. Another sister gave me a "no soliciting" sign several years ago because she noticed we were always getting solicitors at our door. To this day, I can't hang it by my front door. I think of little Lisa Downs going door to door with her wares and I welcome anyone who comes to our door. Thanks, Debbie, for teaching me real compassion at such a young age.

journal a gift

SHE TAUGHT ME by Lisa Bearnson

"Today you are YOU, that is truer than TRUE. There is no one ALIVE who is YOUER than you." —DR. SEUSS

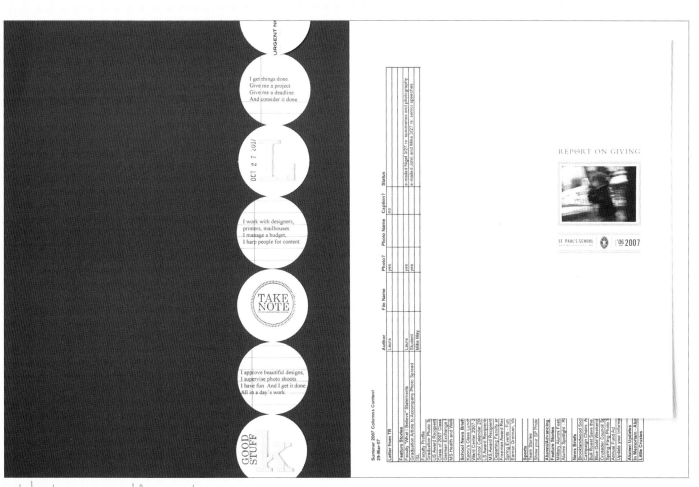

celebrate career achievements

TAKE NOTE by Laura Kurz

It has been almost 5 months since your Great Grandma passed away after 81 years of life. We miss her like crazy, but have been blessed with many reminders of her in our home, including her piano. Grammy remembers when her dad gave this piano as a gift to her mom over 45 years ago. She can remember watching her mom play, and being amazed at how fast her fingers would move across the keys. It was your Great Grandma's escape from the pressures of being a working mother of seven children. Grammy would've loved to learn to play her mom's piano, but never had the opportunity.

share family talents

GRANDMA'S GIFT by Cindy Tobey

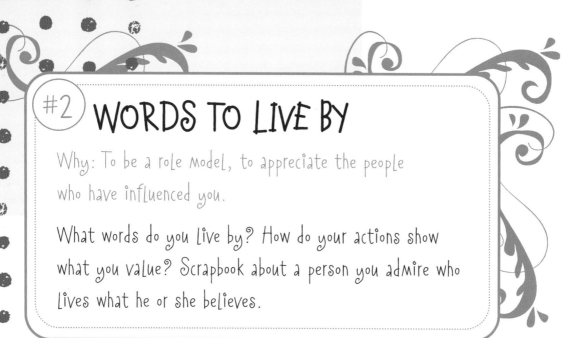

#2 WORDS TO LIVE BY

Why: To be a role model, to appreciate the people who have influenced you.

What words do you live by? How do your actions show what you value? Scrapbook about a person you admire who lives what he or she believes.

DOWN

1. Be _____. Even if you're not, pretend to be. No one can tell the difference.

2. Never remind someone of a kindness or act of _____ you have shown him or her. Bestow a favor and forget it.

4. _____. There is immeasurable power in it.

5. Never underestimate the power of a _____ word or deed.

7. _____ deeply and passionately. You might get hurt, but it's the only way to live life completely.

8. Never deprive someone of _____; it might be all they have.

11. Live a good, _____ life. Then when you get older and think back, you'll get to enjoy it a second time.

ACROSS

3. Never give up on anybody. _____ happen every day.

6. Think big thoughts, but _____ small pleasures.

9. Never waste an _____ to tell someone you love them.

10. Leave everything a little _____ than you found it.

12. Life will sometimes hand you a magical moment. _____ it.

No. 12

words to live by

list defining words

WORDS by Deena Wuest

"It's NICE to be important, BUT it's more IMPORTANT to be nice." —ANONYMOUS

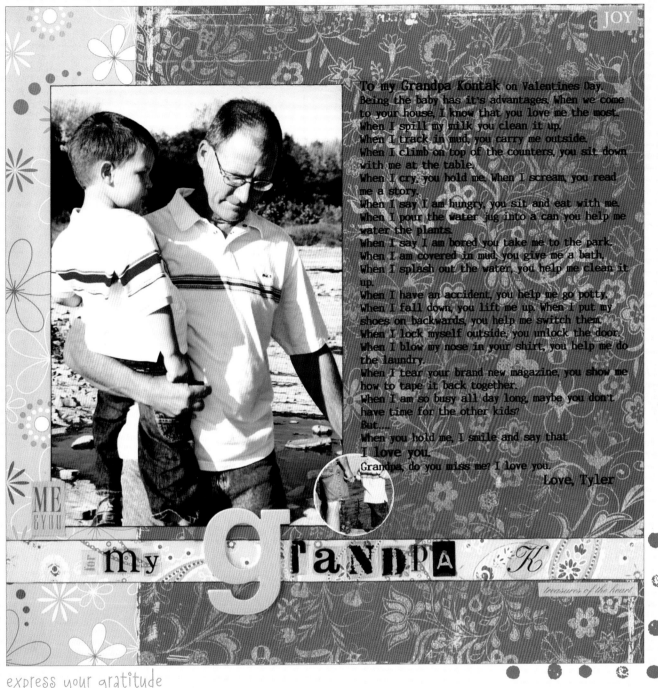

To my Grandpa Kontak on Valentines Day.
Being the baby has it's advantages. When we come
to your house, I know that you love me the most.
When I spill my milk you clean it up.
When I track in mud, you carry me outside.
When I climb on top of the counters, you sit down
with me at the table.
When I cry, you hold me. When I scream, you read
me a story.
When I say I am hungry, you sit and eat with me.
When I pour the water jug into a can you help me
water the plants.
When I say I am bored you take me to the park.
When I am covered in mud, you give me a bath,
When I splash out the water, you help me clean it
up.
When I have an accident, you help me go potty.
When I fall down, you lift me up. When I put my
shoes on backwards, you help me switch them.
When I lock myself outside, you unlock the door.
When I blow my nose in your shirt, you help me do
the laundry.
When I tear your brand new magazine, you show me
how to tape it back together.
When I am so busy all day long, maybe you don't
have time for the other kids?
But....
When you hold me, I smile and say that
I love you.
Grandpa, do you miss me? I love you.

Love, Tyler

ME & YOU

for my **g**r**a**n**d**p**a** *K*

treasures of the heart

express your gratitude

MY GRANDPA K by Jamie Harper

This I know to be true and are the words I strive to live by... "And now I would that ye should be humble, and be submissive and gentle; easy to be entreated; full of patience and long-suffering; being temperate in all things; being diligent in keeping the commandments of God at all times; asking for whatsoever things ye stand in need, both spiritual and temporal; always returning thanks unto God for whatsoever things ye do receive. And see that ye have faith, hope, and charity, and then ye will always abound in good works." This scripture is found in Alma 7:23-24. I have memorized these words and constantly think about them throughout the day. Truly wisdom to live by.

TRUTH

discuss important values

TRUTH by Lisa Bearnson

"Be who you are and SAY what you feel
because those who MIND don't matter and
those who MATTER don't mind." —DR. SEUSS

A FEW THOUGHTS

- One of my GREATEST heroes is my father. He's been a WONDERFUL friend, mentor and example of GOODNESS. When I was 16, I CRASHED through our GARAGE with the family car. My dad came running outside thinking the house was caving in. He ran over to me, gave me a big HUG and said, "Remember, PEOPLE are worth more THAN things."

- It's SO important to extend respect to everyone. Respect your TEACHERS for their wisdom; respect your LEADERS for the wise THOUGHTS they have to OFFER you. Respect the people you MEET each day; you never know how they might teach or LEAD you.

- Every night before I go to bed, I SNEAK inside each of my children's ROOMS to make SURE they're tucked in for the night. I always reflect on their lives and how fast they are growing up. I NEVER leave without saying a LITTLE prayer, pleading THAT they'll be safe from harm.

- SOMETIMES you'll FIND that the very best ADVENTURES happen in your own backyard. ONE of my favorite memories is my entire family washing CARS together and how it ended up in a HUGE friendly water fight!

- EVERYTHING you do throughout the day is a choice. WHAT time you get up, what you eat for breakfast, the CLOTHES you wear, the music you listen to, whether YOU'RE on time or late. Make sure your CHOICES reflect who you are and the life you want TO live.

#3 THE PERFECT ADVENTURE

Why: To share your good memories with others, to remember your relaxing moments.

What's the best vacation you've ever taken? Where do you dream of traveling? What's your perfect escape?

document dream vacations

STARS IN HER EYES by Francine Clouden

"My FAVORITE thing is to GO where I have never GONE." —DIANE ARBUS

explain your escape

SUMMER ESCAPE by Summer Fullerton

Notice how Candice grouped her photographs together into a square. The ribbon at the top of the photographs gives the square the look of an old-fashioned house, which is something you'd discover in Williamsburg.

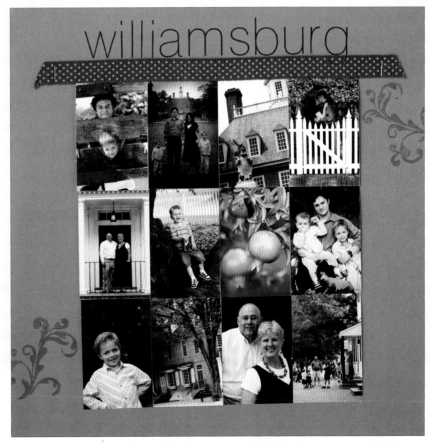

arrange an adventure

WILLIAMSBURG by Candice Stringham

#4 YOU CAN

Why: To reflect your true personality, to share family traits.

What's your attitude toward life, toward your family, friends and career? How do others' attitudes influence your life? How has your attitude changed over time?

I love the fact that you are full to the brim *and overflowing* with confidence, Mika. Having only just met cousin, Sam, you were more than happy to jump in his car and accompany him to the rugby club. Apparently you kicked a ball and ran round happily discovering while he completed his jobs!! A couple of hours later you returned and were the best of mates as he tried to teach you some guitar playing skills. Oh! the places you will go with that attribute, Mika. I love that about you.

Sam and Mika on their verandah in Upper Hutt.   Apr. 07

DREAM

FOLLOW YOUR HEART attribute
YOU CAN DO ANYTHING

HAPPY

showcase special skills

ATTRIBUTE by Hera Frei

Whether YOU think that you CAN,
OR that you can't, YOU
are USUALLY right." —HENRY FORD

It didn't seem to matter that she was a fraction of their age and size. When Anna came to visit she soon had her big cousins wrapped around her finger. It wasn't a magical kind of thing, she just innocently placed her requests or simply took their hand and led them to where she wanted to go. The boys were happy to comply. Then again, maybe there is a bit of magic to this girl after all.

there's a GIRL in the house

and everyone knows who's IN CHARGE

focus on personality

THERE'S A GIRL IN THE HOUSE by Terri Davenport

professional

first bouquet – june 1988

most recent october 2005

Apparently, catching the bouquet is one wedding tradition that is a hoax! Isn't the fair lady who grabs the flowers supposed to be the next to tie the knot? Here I am, 8 or 9 bouquets later (I've seriously lost count!), and still nothing. I've caught them in two countries (the first was in Canada – see picture above), and at least four states and three time zones that I can remember. At first I found it exhilarating: a competition and the spotlight on me for a few fleeting moments. But now...Now it's just too easy! I've actually given up trying – I know the tradition behind the bouquet toss and after 8 (or is it 9?) times – I'm just not buying it!

keep it fun

PROFESSIONAL BOUQUET CATCHER by Susan Opel

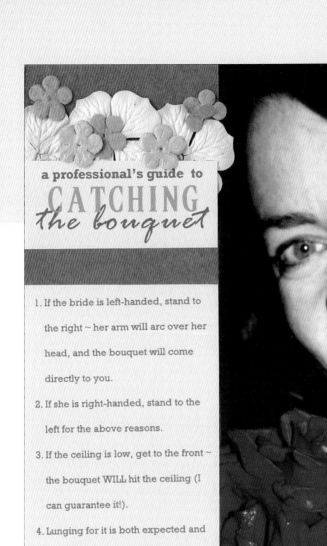

a professional's guide to
CATCHING
the bouquet

1. If the bride is left-handed, stand to the right ~ her arm will arc over her head, and the bouquet will come directly to you.

2. If she is right-handed, stand to the left for the above reasons.

3. If the ceiling is low, get to the front ~ the bouquet WILL hit the ceiling (I can guarantee it!).

4. Lunging for it is both expected and acceptable – just don't fall!

5. A nine-year-old boy catches the garter 8 times out of 10.

Fabulous

bouquet *catcher*

#5 IT'S A BALANCING ACT

Why: To think about your true priorities, to remind others that balance is crucial.

How do you keep your life balanced? What does the concept of balance mean to you? What are your top three priorities (or do you know)?

share your strategies

GOOD BETTER BEST by Lisa Bearnson

Here, Amanda journals about her struggles to find balance in her various life roles. This layout is a reminder of her favorite advice: that she must take good care of herself to take good care of others.

LATELY, NATHAN'S been CRAZY BUSY AT WORK AND I'VE been ON MY OWN WITH THIS WHOLE PARENTING THING MUCH MORE THAN NORMAL. IT'S been A STRUGGLE FOR ME AND HAS DEFINITELY GIVEN ME A WHOLE NEW RESPECT FOR SINGLE PARENTS EVERYWHERE. IN TRYING TO PINPOINT THINGS THAT COULD HELP, I CAME TO REALIZE THAT WHAT I WAS MISSING MOST WAS MY DAILY DOSE OF SANITY. YOU SEE, NORMALLY, WHEN NATHAN GETS HOME FROM WORK, I HAVE THE OPPORTUNITY TO RETREAT ON MY OWN FOR A BIT... TO REGROUP AND TAKE A PARENTING BREAK WHILE NATHAN AND THE BOYS RECONNECT. I COUNT ON THAT TIME AT THE END OF THE DAY. I NEED IT FOR MYSELF. I KNOW THAT SOME MIGHT FEEL GUILTY FOR ADMITTING THAT, BUT I DON'T. ACTUALLY, ONE OF THE BEST PIECES OF ADVICE I PICKED UP BEFORE HAVING KIDS WAS TO REMEMBER TO TAKE CARE OF MYSELF. IF I'M NOT DOING WELL, I'M JUST NOT GOING TO FUNCTION AS WELL AS A PARENT. SO, TAKING THIS DAILY TIME FOR MYSELF IS SOMETHING THAT I ACTUALLY DO WITH MY SONS IN MIND. I AM A BETTER MOMMY WHEN I FEEL MORE FULFILLED AND HEALTHY AS AN INDIVIDUAL. SO, WHEN I SEE A PICTURE LIKE THIS OF MY GUYS ALL HANGING OUT TOGETHER, I AM HAPPY. IT MEANS I'M NOT IN THE MIDDLE OF THINGS AND AM FREE TO DO WHAT I WANT FOR A BIT. IF THAT MEANS I'M BUSILY SNAPPING PICTURES OF THIS "FREE" TIME, SO BE IT.

Other things I do for myself to be a better parent:

I stay up after they've gone to bed to work on my own projects.

I run errands without them when Nathan is home.

I read books (without talking trains or time traveling kids) when I can.

I go on "dates" with Nathan once a month.

I proclaim "mommy time" and shut the door to my office (though I can see and hear through it).

I exercise regularly and request no interruptions.

I scrapbook.

journal your priorities
DAILY DOSE by Amanda Probst

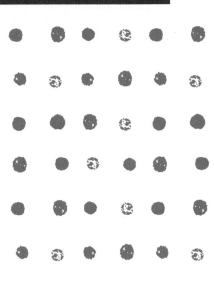

show what's important

BALANCING by Lisa Brown

family
friends
work sleep
hobbies
housework

NCING

THEY SAY THAT YOU CAN'T HAVE IT ALL AND I HAVE TO AGREE. NO MATTER HOW WELL I TRY TO SCHEDULE AND PLAN I NEVER HAVE ENOUGH TIME TO DO EVERY THING THAT I WANT. IT'S A CONSTANT BALANCING ACT.

"BALANCE is beautiful." —MIYOKO OHNO

looking

I recently had one of those moments. Ya know, the kind of moment where you leave your body and feel like you're an outsider looking in? Well, that's the kind of moment I had. And I saw a woman. Barefoot. Pregnant. A little girl tugging on her shirt. A toddler wrapped around her leg. Chopping vegetables in the kitchen. The floor resembled that of a movie theatre and a mysterious brown substance (what one could only hope was chocolate pudding) graced a cabinet door. The teenager in me would have taken one look at that sight and rolled her eyes. She would have seen a woman who is wasting her life. She would have seen lost dreams and shackles of responsibility. She would have seen no connection to the well dressed woman in a penthouse that she imagined would be her future. But the picture I saw was something completely different. I saw a home overflowing with love. I saw a woman who was truly happy and fulfilled in her life. A woman who felt beautiful carrying an extra 30 pounds. A little girl who was sharing the adventures of her day at bible school and a toddler who was squeezing his mommy's leg screaming, "I love you! I like you!" A floor sticky with "Pepsi Diet" and a cabinet that held evidence of the brownies the family made the night before. As I snapped back into the moment, I stopped. I looked around. I tried to memorize every sight...every sound. For THIS is life at it's greatest. So full of love and blessings that they pour out the windows. So that penthouse? Ya, you can keep that.

find the beauty

LOOKING IN by Deena Wuest

A Little Birdie told Me...

you're beautiful {yes you}

My brown-eyed girl, I know this has been a tough year for you. You get so upset and cry when the boys call you "Miss Moley"... ....what you don't know is that those boys are the ones that will go "GA GA" for that beauty-mark of yours when you're older! Your beauty mark is special, it's what sets you apart. You're beautiful! ♥ mom

write a love note

YOU'RE BEAUTIFUL by Jeni Boisvert

" Beauty comes in ALL sizes, NOT just size 5. " —ROSEANNE BARR

feeling good in my own skin

accept yourself today

FEELING GOOD IN MY OWN SKIN by Lisa Bearnson

This is Me!

My hair rarely looks perfectly coiffed. I only wash and style it every four days. I'd rather spend the time with my family than primping in the mirror.

The wrinkles on my forehead represent wisdom, maturity and a little worry!

I know it sounds crazy but I'm okay with my never-will-be-totally-flat again stomach. Heck- I'm proud that for 36 months (that's three years!) it housed my four biggest blessings.

I have "mom" hands. They are practical and functional. My nails aren't long or perfectly manicured. My hands are wrinkled, dry and my fingers have lots of those little cracks that hurt. I love my hands because they do lots of useful things. They braid hair, push a swing, drive a carpool to school, make yummy cookies, put Bandaids on boo-boos and hug kids good night.

My legs will never run in a marathon. But they will continue to valiantly run this race called life. They will jump on trampolines, take a hot meal to a sick neighbor and walk by your side!

"Happiness comes from accepting the bodies we have been given as divine gifts and enhancing our natural attributes, not from remaking our bodies after the image of the world."
Susan W. Tanner

"You're in PRETTY good shape for the SHAPE you're in." —DR. SEUSS

(#7) BELIEVE

Why: To give people perspective on your actions, to reflect on your beliefs.

What do you believe? How has your faith influenced your life? How have your family's beliefs been passed along to you?

celebrate childhood innocence

WHY THE WORLD NEEDS SUPERMAN by Jamie Harper

> "Sometimes I've BELIEVED as MANY as six IMPOSSIBLE things before breakfast."
>
> —LEWIS CARROLL, ALICE IN WONDERLAND

LIVE in the NOW

You're never very far apart when you're holding hands.

This I learned from you

Riches are in the heart, not the pocketbook.

Be humble and gentle.

Pray always

Home can be a heaven on earth through love, hard work, unselfishness, and complete acceptance.

Stick together

Live your religion 24 hours a day, seven days a week.

Be a good example at all times and in all places.

Strive for excellence, not perfection.

Say "I love you" every day.

People are worth more than things.

document family values

LIVE IN THE NOW by Lisa Bearnson

#8 PASSIONS

Why: To define yourself outside of your traditional roles, to remind yourself of what makes you happy.

What are you passionate about? What are your family members passionate about? How did you discover your passions, and how have they played out in your life?

By far, one of Jason's favorite things to do is reading! Whatever extra time he finds goes into this passion. When I asked Jason what types of books he reads, he said "I love Science Fiction, Fantasy, Comics, and sometimes Mystery/Suspense".

Jason's long time love of reading comes from his Mother. He said, that as a kid his Mom loved to read a lot. Her passion, rubbed off on him at a very young age. Jason loves that books can take him to a different place and time.

As a child his first memories of reading were of sitting in his playpen, surrounded by toys, reading about Charlie Brown's troubles in Peanuts® books.

Type of Books He Reads

- □ 1%
- □ 5%
- □ 9%
- □ 85%

□ Science Fiction ■ Comics □ Fantasy □ Mystery/Suspense

HOOKED ON BOOKS

graph a hobby

HOOKED ON BOOKS by Heidi Sonboul

discover your passion

PASSION FOUND by Jamie Harper

"Nothing GREAT in this world has ever been ACCOMPLISHED WITHOUT passion."
—FRIEDRICH HEBBEL

express your love

LOVE IT by Candice Stringham

#9 BE AWARE OF WONDER

Why: To make a wish list, to ask questions and seek the answers.

What are you curious about? What do you want to know more about? What intrigues you and makes you really think?

ponder the possibilities

OUR CONNECTION by Elizabeth Kartchner

"Sometimes QUESTIONS are more important than ANSWERS." —NANCY WILLARD

Yes, I have a sweet tooth. So do people all over the world, as it turns out. When we went to EPCOT, I decided I wanted to buy candy, cookies, or some other form of deliciousness from all of the pavilions in the World Showcase (except for America... pretty much already know what American candy tastes like). And I was able to find something tasty in every country except for Morocco... maybe they just don't like candy. Whatever. It's been really exciting to sample the goods since returning from our trip. I've learned, for example, that the Chinese 'White Rabbit' candy is just gross. I mean seriously, it tastes like nothing. And the Japanese candy counter had a dizzying assortment, each more colorful than the last. My favorite so far have been the Italian fruit gems. On the other hand, I haven't been brave enough to try the Mexican goat milk candy yet. On the whole, though, it's been an eye-opening (and tooth-rotting) experience.

try something new

I WANT CANDY by Joni Lynn

#10 CHANGE

Why: To remind yourself that you can accept changes, to gain confidence to tackle new things.

How do you handle change in your life? How have you handled transitions like moving, changing schools, entering a new relationship, getting married, starting a new job?

It was a year of events – events that changed the course of my life once and for all.

January: I was invited to an art workshop in Bangalore – those few weeks made me realize art is my REFUGE.

February-May: I collected data for my Masters thesis and got to meet many contemporary artists.

June-August: Completed my Masters degree in Clinical Psychology with flying colors. Applied for my PhD.

September: I turned 25. My parents arranged my wedding with a complete stranger, Ashis.

October: I took one last vacation with my parents. Got stranded due to bad storm.

November: Got married to Ashis.

December: Packed my essentials in one suitcase and moved to the US with Ashis.

and I was never going to be the same again...

record landmark experiences

1999 by Mou Saha

The way our family came together in March, 2006, is nothing short of a miracle. After several years of trying to have a baby, your Dad and I thought we might never have a family. We had always talked about adopting older children as an option, and the day my Mom, your Grandma S., told us about you, this option suddenly became very real.

You were eight and nine years old and living with your Nanny, who just happened to go to Grandma and Grandpa S' church. Nanny had cancer for the second time. She wouldn't get better. There was no one else to take care of you and she was praying for a miracle. Did we want to meet you? Honestly, we had to think about it for a few days. This was a big commitment - we didn't know what you two had been through, only that your past was very troubled. Ultimately, it was a decision we just had to make with our hearts. How could we say no?

Our first meeting was after church on a Sunday afternoon. We hit it off so well, it was like we had always known you. This was definitely meant to be. We met you several times over the next few weeks and also visited your Nanny in the hospital many times to talk to her about the future. Everyone agreed that this was right, and so Nanny wrote in her will that she wanted us to be your guardians after she was gone.

You moved in with us only six weeks after we first met. Nanny passed away peacefully two months later. She had received her miracle. We received a miracle too.

The Story of Us

"We did not CHANGE as we grew older; WE just became more CLEARLY ourselves."
—LYNN HALL

celebrate a new family

THE STORY OF US by Lisa Habisreutinger

what's in a name baby?

grandma = LOVE

I'm trying to figure out my grandma name
Do I look like a grandma* or a gran*?
Or do I look more like a maemae* or a
granny* a g-ma* or a nanna*
or a nan*? One thing is certain,
whatever name I choose, will be filled with

love

explore changing relationships

WHAT'S IN A NAME, BABY? by Cheryl Nelson

#11 MY HERO

Why: To aspire toward exceptional qualities, to celebrate those people who motivate or inspire you.

Who is your hero? How are you your own hero? Why do we need heroes in our lives?

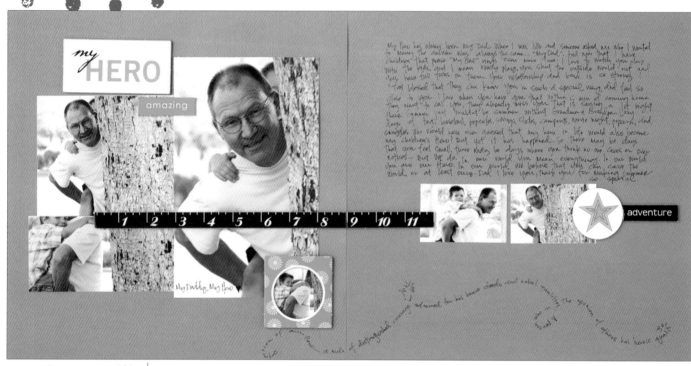

journal your gratitude

MY HERO by Jamie Harper

"A HERO is no braver than an ordinary man, but he is BRAVER five MINUTES longer." —RALPH WALDO EMERSON

I had an amazing childhood filled with fun and laughter, but nothing could prepare me for my share of heartaches and the roller coaster ride that was to follow. But life has come full circle. I am blessed with love and happiness.

full circle

be the hero

FULL CIRCLE by Nisha Morton

#12 LEARN FROM A CHILD

Why: To look at your life with an honest, joyful, fresh perspective; to remind yourself not to take life so seriously all the time.

How would a child describe your life? How have children enriched your life? Tell a funny story about innocent comments a child has made about your life.

A moment ago,
your heart beat under mine.

Now, I can touch your chest and feel your actual heartbeat.

A moment ago,
your feet were lodged beneath my ribs.

Now, your feet are nestled in my hands as I count each precious toe.

A moment ago,
I couldn't imagine what you'd look like...what you'd feel like.

Now, I can hold you in my arms, take in your sweet face and touch your petal soft skin.

A moment ago,
I could no longer stand the pain.

Now, I stand in awe of our awesome and gracious God.

Amazing how a single **moment** can change everything

cherish Magic Moments

A SINGLE MOMENT by Deena Wuest

sweet GIRL

Mom, im sorey I bin Bad. I Love you, Love Sage

All I really need to know I learned through Sage Adeline Bearnson. **Always be the first to say you're sorry when you hurt somebody.** I recently came home to this adorable "I'm sorry" letter lovingly placed on my bed. Sage and I had a little disagreement earlier in the afternoon and she was the first to say she was sorry. **Never leave the house without a kiss, a hug and saying "I Love You."** No matter how big of a hurry she's in, Sage always takes the time to make us feel loved. **Sing in the shower.** We always know Sage's in the bathroom when she's singing at the top of her lungs. **Love who you are.** As we were snuggling one night, Sage looked up at me and said, "Have you noticed how I really care for other people and feel bad when someone is sad or hurt?" I love how Sage already knows her strengths and abilities and isn't afraid to share them. **Don't take life too seriously.** Sometimes in my quest for excellence, I try too hard with the housecleaning, laundry and doing Sage's hair. On the occasions when I get frustrated because I'm trying to do it all, Sage just looks at me and says, "Oh Well, Mom." I'm trying to adapt this simple "Oh Well" statement into my own life. It is what it is and it's important to just try your best. **Play hard and have fun.** The end!

share sweet thoughts

SWEET GIRL by Lisa Bearnson

"A child REMINDS us that playtime is an ESSENTIAL part of our daily routine."
—ANONYMOUS

HAPPY BIRTHDAY TAYLOR MAY YOUR DAY BE FILLED WITH AS MANY WONDERFUL SURPRISES AS YOU HAVE GIVEN *me.*

of all the gifts i've been given, you're the best! blow out the candles *Beautiful*

THEN & NOW

happy happy happy

happy happy happy happy happy happy happy happy

{party}

Taylor, I am amazed at how quickly the years have gone by. You are so strong, and have grown into quite the young woman. I am proud of you, Happy Birthday.

remember special birthdays

THEN AND NOW by Jamie Harper

(#13) A WISH THAT CAME TRUE

Why: To remember that wishes do come true, to appreciate even the small things that happen for you.

Write about a wish that came true for you. What was the wish? How long did it take for your wish to come true?

a wish come true

Mom got a new leash on life after I was born. The pain of losing her first baby and the mounting wall of depression around her began to melt away as she immersed herself in me. Every obstacle she faced in her new venture became a wish — a wish for me to never have to face those challenges, a wish for me to have better chances. She wanted me to grow up to be a well-rounded person and took me to school, art class, swimming and gymnastics practices. Transportation services were inadequate, inconvenient and expensive and owning a car was not common. We walked for miles, sometimes for hours. After a whole hectic day of school and sports, I often fell asleep and mom had to carry me home along with the baggage. I cannot even imagine the extent of her exhaustion but never heard her complain. All she ever said was, 'Wish we could afford a car, any small car... how much could those tiny feet take!' Then years flew by, I got married. Now, we have two cars to go places. We hardly walk anymore. And my mom? Well, her wish came true... Her child and grandchildren do not have that disadvantage anymore. And she thanks God everyday for granting her wish and for her wonderful son-in-law who made it all happen.

India circa 1976

remember the wish

A WISH COME TRUE by Mou Saha

"A dream is a WISH YOUR heart makes." —CINDERELLA

It's so much fun to see how Marci included photographs of her children as babies and at their current ages on this layout. I love being able to compare photographs at different stages of their lives.

tell three wishes

3 WISHES COME TRUE by Marci Leishman

celebrate a child

CHLOE by Emily Magelby

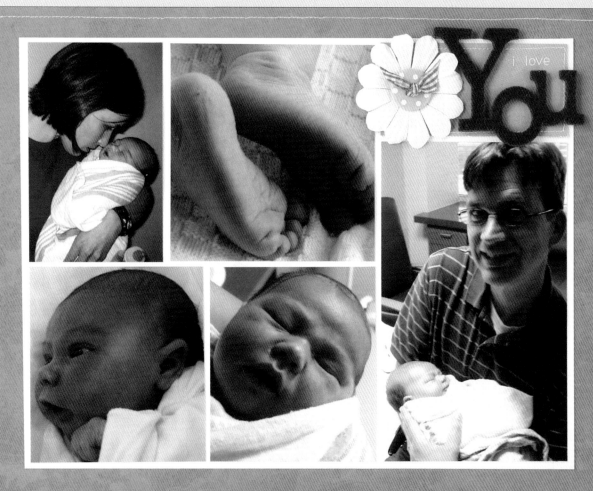

i knew the minute i saw you that all my wishes and dreams had come true. i really had a daughter, and you were perfect in every way. you were so healthy and alert and would stare right into my eyes. i could never have imagined my love for you would be so strong - i thought my heart would burst. after everything we had been through, to know you were in my arms was pure magic.

so, to my dear, sweet chloe i want you to know that i adore you and i am so glad that Heavenly Father has let me be your mommy.

chloe jane · first week · june 2007

"When you LOVE someone, all your saved up WISHES START coming out." —Elizabeth Bowen

(#14) COMMUNITY SPIRIT

Why: To feel a connection to other people, to recall precious memories of what it was like growing up in your hometown.

Journal about the community spirit where you live.
How do people pull together in times of happiness or sadness?
How do you fit in as a member of your community?

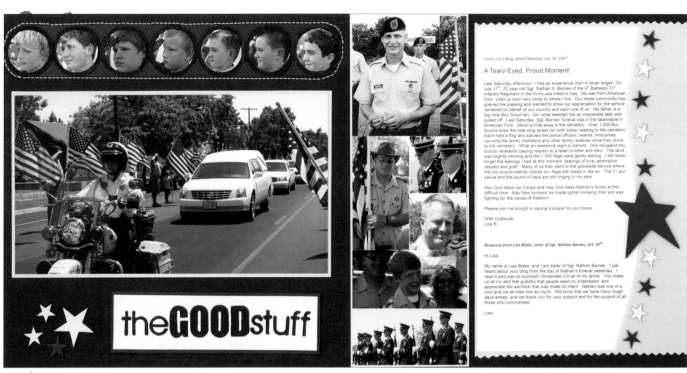

celebrate community connections

THE GOOD STUFF by Lisa Bearnson

"The UNIVERSAL brotherhood of MAN is our most precious POSSESSION." —MARK TWAIN

Beth had just as much fun capturing the photographs for this layout as she did creating it, and it shows on this page. Take a day and photograph as many items as you can to show your favorite team (or hobby or place or people.)

Colts win
Super Bowl!
Indianapolis
goes wild!
2007

show your spirit

SUPER! by Beth Opel

(#15) COMFORT FOOD

Why: To remember warm memories, to find comfort in what nourishes you.

What's your comfort food? Why is it your comfort food? In what ways does it comfort you, and why?

cup cakes

we love cupcakes, especially with sprinkles. the lambert girls are all bakers and cupcakes are our specialty.

october 07

awesome

recall family favorites

CUPCAKES by Marci Lambert

"Food, like a LOVING touch or a glimpse of DIVINE power, has the ability to COMFORT."

—NORMAN KOLPAS

comfort food   10-26-05

Welcome Home, Kids!

I missed You!

Growing up, my mom always had an afternoon snack waiting when we came through the door. We were often greeted with the smell of fresh-baked bread or cinnamon rolls. It really didn't matter what the snack was. What did matter was the sense of incredible stability and comfort I felt from this simple act. I knew mom was there to take away the cares of the day. I've continued this tradition with my own children. Sometimes I make banana chocolate chip muffins, other times it's bought cookies. Everyone agrees the afternoon snack is the best comfort food in the world. P.S. I have a cute white board where I write a special note.

share comforting traditions

COMFORT FOOD by Lisa Bearnson

(#16) PERSONALITY

Why: To remember your strengths, to share who you are.

What's your personality? How do others describe you? How does the spirited personality of your child (or a family member or friend) affect your life?

present personality traits

BIG PRESENCE by Lori Mar

"It is BEAUTY which captures your attention; PERSONALITY which CAPTURES your heart." —UNKNOWN

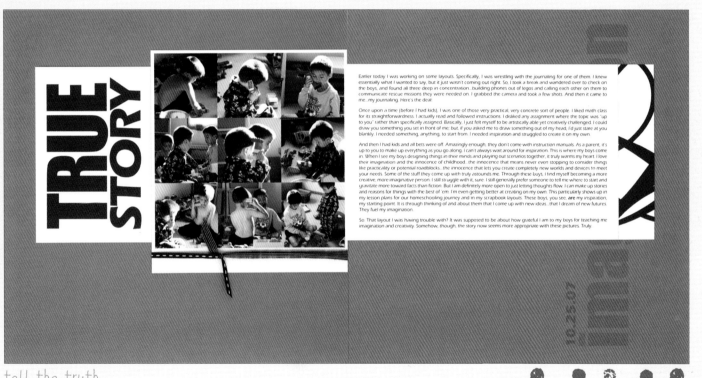

tell the truth

TRUE STORY by Amanda Probst

(#17) COURAGE

Why: To remember that you can overcome, to help others meet challenges without fear.

What do you fear? How do you face your fears?

Worrying... wondering... waiting for Steve to land on safe ground after his solo flight. I felt nervous and anxious.
The necklace I'm wearing gives me hope. Its simple message says "I will follow God's plan for me."
I must continue to trust in the Lord. I must put my life in

His hands. I must keep the faith that Steve will return home safe and sound.
October 2007

SOLO

seek spiritual comfort

SOLO by Lisa Bearnson

"Yesterday I dared to struggle, today I DARE to WIN." —BERNADETTE DEVLIN

worry

Maybe it was my difficult pregnancies, the fact that we had to work so hard to get you here, but I am the worst kind of worrier. I lie awake at night wondering what might happen to you when you go off to school by yourself or when you're riding your bike on the sidewalk. I worry about things I have no control over and I worry about silly things like whether or not you've taken a long enough nap today. Jackson, you took the brunt of most of my worrying...being the first child, you've had to suffer me hovering over you at the playground and being a control freak about everything. Brady, you're lucky because seeing Jackson grow into a wonderful little boy has made me worry less and helped me to not be so over-protective. What I know now is that you both have to learn by doing and I can't hold you back because I'm worried. You're going to make mistakes, you're going to fall down and get bumps and bruises, you're heart will get broken, but that these things will happen whether I worry about them or not. One day at a time, I'm learning to let go.

24/7

overcome your worries

WORRY by Kelly Noel

Remember

Where

face the fear

WHERE WERE YOU? by Summer Ford

were you ?

Where were you when the world stopped turning that September day?

This line, from the gut wrenching song written by Alan Jackson shortly after 9-11, stops me in my tracks every time I hear it. The world as I had always knew it changed that day. For the first time in my life I felt unsafe in my own home.

Did you stand there in shock at the site of
That black smoke rising against that blue sky
Did you shout out in anger
In fear for your neighbor
Or did you just sit down and cry

I did all of the above. The first visions of the horrific events were watched in jaw dropping awe, the tears soon followed, and the anger still lives within and rises to the surface sometimes.

Did you weep for the children
Who lost their dear loved ones
And pray for the ones who don't know
Did you rejoice for the people who walked from the rubble
And sob for the ones left below

I also wept for my own two children at the time. Holt was two and Hunter just four months old. The fact that they will never know a world without 9-11 saddens me. The tragedy is relived on television every year since but at the same time, the heroes emerge stronger and more glorious as time passes.

Did you burst out in pride
For the red white and blue
The heroes who died just doing what they do
Did you look up to heaven for some kind of answer
And look at yourself to what really matters

The sight of every house on our block with America flags flying proudly will never be forgotten. American pride at its very best.

But I know Jesus and I talk to God
And I remember this from when I was young
Faith hope and love are some good things he gave us
And the greatest is love

It is love for our country that brought us to our knees that day. It is the love for our families that keeps us moving forward, and it is the love of GOD that brings us peace within our hearts.

Did you go to a church and hold hands with some stranger
Stand in line and give your own blood
Did you just stay home and cling tight to your family
Thank God you had somebody to love

I will never forget sitting with my children, hugging them and telling how sorry I was. I could not wait for my husband to get home and for the four of us to hold each other close.

Where were you when the world stopped turning that September day?

9-11

(#18) CREATE AND IMAGINE

Why: To tap into the creative essence of your personality, to open your eyes to possibilities.

How are you creative? What do you imagine for yourself? How do you express your creativity and imagination?

document creative opportunities

BEAUTY by Yvette Adams

I love how Laura included one of her early works of art on this page and used it as a way to discuss her current artistic talents.

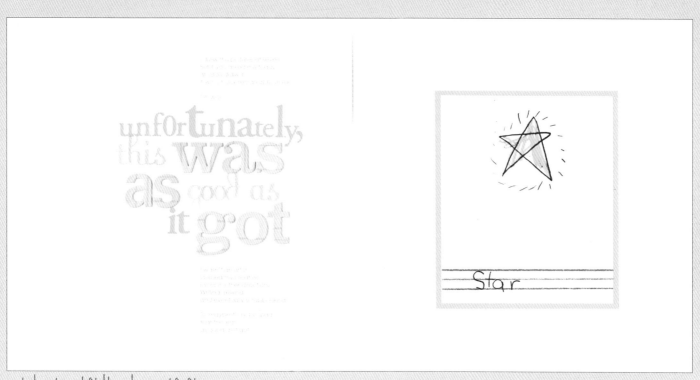

celebrate childhood creativity

AS GOOD AS IT GOT by Laura Kurz

"THERE IS NO ONE ALIVE WHO IS YOUER THAN YOU"

DR SEUSS

express your vision

THERE IS NO ONE... by Elizabeth Kartchner

Who would think DR. Seuss could be inspiring? Not me. But he is. I found this quote online one day & immediately wrote it down & hung it up in my office. I had been a little down lately and this was just what I needed to hear.

I made a resolution that in the times when I get down on myself think about my strengths & what defines me. Being small doesn't bring any good to life! Be grateful for who I am.

It reminded me to be me!! And all that entails. Be the silly, genuine, sentimental, indecisive, happy girl I am. The girl who loves the simple moments of each day. Who sings at the top of her lungs in the car, makes cupcakes to bring to a friend, does yoga to clear her mind who writes down goals often to grow & know who she wants to be.

Be you- it's what you do best! Be thoughtful, loving, silly, and analytical.

"The WORLD is but a CANVAS to the IMAGINATION." —HENRY DAVID THOREAU

#19 MAKE THE CHOICE

Why: To show how the choices you've made have influenced your life, to help future generations understand the power of choice.

What choices do you make on a daily basis? How do you make your choices (i.e., what's your process)? Do you like making decisions or dislike it?

NAME _____ FOLIO _____ 71

BOX NUMBERS 1 2 3 4 5 6 7 8 9 10 11 12 13 14 TOTAL

not the PoPular Choice

It was the Friday before Homecoming weekend. Kade's 11th grade math teacher told the class that she was going to give them a break because of Homecoming—they could skip a chapter so they wouldn't have homework over the weekend. Kade raised his hand and said, "We really need to learn this chapter so we'll do well in our math college classes and on the ACT test. My suggestion is to not skip this section and give us the homework." It was dead silent in the room—everyone was shocked by Kade's comment. Mrs. Hutsman, the teacher, then took a class vote and the majority of the students agreed with Kade and wanted the homework assignment. Mrs. Hutsman told me about this incident at parent teacher conference. She was very impressed by Kade's willingness to speak up!

make the choice

NOT THE POPULAR CHOICE by Lisa Bearnson

"It is our CHOICES . . . that SHOW what we TRULY are, far more than OUR abilities." —J. K. ROWLING

share your philosophies

THERE IS ALWAYS A CHOICE by Mou Saha

⃝#20 DISCOVERY

Why: To share your joy in discovering new things, to remind yourself to never stop seeking

What do you take joy in discovering? What would you like to discover about yourself or in others? What's one thing you've discovered about yourself in the last week?

find the unexpected

NORCAL by Caroline Ikeji

"No pessimist EVER discovered the SECRET of the stars or SAILED an uncharted land, OR opened a new doorway for the HUMAN spirit." —HELEN KELLER

HARD

THINGS

Elder Cook told our youth, while visiting Stake Conference last fall, that they can do "hard things". At the time, I thought "okay, he is talking to the youth, how can I encourage them, how can I remind them of this, how can they know that they really can do hard things."

But throughout the year, I have learned that I too can do hard things. My hard things are not the same as the youth today, I won't be tempted like they are or put myself in some of their same situations, but I will have hard things to overcome and triumph over.

I have my own "hard things". Things out of my comfort zone. I am the Young Women's President and I don't like being in front of people or in charge of or responsible for things. I am a scrapbooker and I sometimes have fast deadlines and difficult products to use. I am a volunteer at Isaac's school, and I don't always have the time or the abilities to make it to his school and take care of my responsibilities. I am a wife and a mother, and I am responsible for their wellbeing and their happiness.

I have discovered as I have put myself in these situations that I can do hard things too.

discover your strengths

HARD THINGS by Jill Orton

Just an hour south of us in Salem is the A.C. Gilbert Museum. The museum is located on the Willamette River. The museum is a series of small houses all connected by a giant play area that includes a massive erector set, a life sized checker board and a spider web climbing structure.

DESTINATION: a.c

explore your world

DESTINATION by Summer Fullerton

You have several favorites at the museum. One is the water works station – you would play in the bubbles all afternoon if I let you.

Another is the recycled art area. It's filled with empty yogurt containers, toilet paper rolls, scraps of fabric, construction paper and all the tape you could want. This is your kind of art – free form and fun.

DATE MONTH YEAR
3 24 05

. gilbert museum . . .

"I DO not SEEK. I find." —PABLO PICASSO

#21 THINK BIG, DREAM BIG!

Why: To make your dreams tangible, to reflect on your hopes.

What are your hopes and dreams? What hopes and dreams have you already realized? How did you make your hopes and dreams come true?

what do you do when opportunity knocks so hard you wake up at night? when you know in your heart you're on the right path but you're afraid? when it's time to decide? what do you do?

i think you have to **say** YES

follow your heart

SAY YES by Marci Lambert

Take a note from Caroline and tell your story in snippets.
These little paper-punched squares are the perfect place
to jot down handwritten journaling comments.

Not a girl, definitely not quite a woman...

realizing that I don't really know what I want to do after all, and hoping to find it soon...

Having a lot of hopes & dreams, but am not quite sure where to start...

Missing writing, and wanting to try to get back into it...

Trying not to take all my blessings for granted...

wondering where life will take me the next few years...

Realizing that time moves way too fast and wanting to take advantage of every single moment...

THIS school thing is dragging out, but I know I'll get there someday, someday!

Searching for my independence... trying to be less dependent...

right now
October 2007

spotlight your story
ME RIGHT NOW by Caroline Ikeji

appreciate the possibilities

ON TOP OF THE WORLD by Susan Weckesser

"Dreams are like STARS —you may never TOUCH them, but if you FOLLOW them, they will LEAD you to your destiny." —UNKNOWN

THOUGHTS ON HOPES AND DREAMS

- I've REALIZED that EVERYTHING in life is a trade-off. When we're watching TV, surfing the Internet, READING a book, talking on the phone or PLAYING video games, we're trading time that we could be doing something else. Are these THINGS worth the portion of our LIVES that we've DEDICATED to them?

- Do you know what YOUR hopes and dreams are? WHAT is important to YOU? What do you want to ACCOMPLISH in your life? Who do you want to be as a PERSON?

- Have you WRITTEN down your goals and POSTED them somewhere so you can see them each DAY? Write them down so you can MAKE them HAPPEN.

- Your hopes and DREAMS don't have to be COMPLEX or impossible to achieve. Even pursuing the SMALLEST dream can add MEANING and INTEREST to your life.

- How much time do you SPEND each day nourishing your HOPES and DREAMS? In today's busy world, it may SEEM as if there's no free time at all, but is there a PLACE where you can MAKE the trade?

- You can do THIS: A friend recently GAVE up her time surfing the Internet to take PAINTING classes. Those CLASSES fill her life with so much JOY and happiness.

#22 ALWAYS KEEP LEARNING

Why: To show how you value education, to teach others the lessons you've learned.

Where did you go to school? Who were your favorite teachers? What's the best thing you learned through formal education?

Just the start of something really good

Victoria I can hardly believe you have graduated from high school. You have just started what will be the rest of your life.

Be strong, stay smart and remember how much we love you. We are so excited to see who you will become.

May, 2007

celebrate new beginnings

GRADUATION by Mary Rogers

"EDUCATION is a kind of continuing dialogue." — ROBERT HUTCHINS

Looking Forward

The road has been long
the end is in sight
I have no more excuses.

The road is scary
I must finish it now
map it out, figure it out
plan it out. NOW.

The road is paved
with classes to take
photography, typography,
Illustrator and more.

The road may be bumpy
but for fear of failure
can't let it stop me from
finishing the degree.

poem by Karen Wilson-Bonnar

choose your path

LOOKING FORWARD by Karen Wilson-Bonnar

SCHOOL stuff everywhere · every e

HOME an observation

p always

art supplies a

must be Love!

I blinked and everywhere I look there is something from homeschooling. Two short years of creeping into every corner! slowly... slowly... then wham! You're surrounded by school stuff. This invasion is not surprizing because if we're not doing school, then I'm thinking/planning about school. When you have two busy elementary kids and a slightly crazy mom/teacher it was bound to happen. A sign of fun and learning. A sign of the joy of being together discovering all sorts of neat (and yes, sometimes boring) things. This is not a complaint though! Just an observation. I'll take the clutter anyday (and that says a lot!)

school stuff tools s

freetime tools f

show your school

HOMESCHOOL STUFF by Kim Spencer

"An EDUCATED man is one who can entertain a NEW idea, ENTERTAIN another PERSON, and entertain himself." —SIDNEY WOOD

planning

library loads

l

I am so blessed to be able to do this adventure with you Avery and Holly. Your stuff may clutter my house ~ but you clutter my heart! I love you!!

manipulatives of every kind

m

u

unit materials in bins

2007

(#23) YOUR BEST IS GOOD ENOUGH

Why: To remind yourself of the importance of trying, to reflect on what excellence means to you.

Give an example of a time when you tried your best. What does excellence mean to you? What do you want excellence to mean to your children?

My sweet boy, now that your speech is finally improving, you've started asking a thousand questions a minute.

"Where Daddy go?" "What happen TV?" "Where book?" They come one after the other with no end in sight. Other mothers might find the endless barrage of questions frustrating, but not me. If there is one lesson I'd want to teach as a parent, it would be to never hesitate before asking questions and to ask more and more.

I have a good friend who is worried that people will think she's stupid, so when I talk to her and she doesn't understand what I am trying to explain, she won't ever admit it. She won't ask any questions. She will just sit there and nod until I stop.

What I wish she would know is that every person has strengths and weaknesses. None of us are perfect at everything. When my friend Ben told his friends that I spoke seven languages, I'd always make sure he also mentioned that I didn't know how to ride a bike.

So, my little boy, hang on to the inquisitive side of yourself and never be too scared to ask questions. Even if the person in front of you is better than you are at that subject, remember that he isn't better at everything and the only way you'll learn is by asking. The only way you'll grow is by asking.

So, ask.

ask excellent questions

ASK by Karen Grunberg

"STRIVE for excellence,
not PERFECTION." —OPRAH WINFREY

your best is good enough

On Brecken's ninth birthday, she competed in a barrel and jumping competition. She'd practiced for many hours before the event and was excited to ride Trouble and compete in front of her family. She and her friend, Lexi, both did an amazing job. When they announced the places, Lexi got first and Brecken got third. You were all smiles for these photos and then exclaimed, "I love the color yellow in this ribbon—it will look so good hanging on my wall." Wow—what a good example for the rest of us to follow. You had done your best and it was definitely good enough. You were excited for Lexi's first place and happy about your third place. Our family motto is: "Strive for excellence, not perfection." In this case you did just that! Great job, Brecken! March 4, 2005.

try your best

YOUR BEST IS GOOD ENOUGH by Lisa Bearnson

Amanda's thought-provoking journaling is a great example of how to create a layout that will teach others your values and help them see your point of view.

Noah asked me the other day what it means to get a "B minus". He'd heard it on a show but had absolutely no concept of how grades work. Hooray! Not that I don't want him to understand grades or endeavor for excellence. Definitely not. But, part of our choice to homeschool involved a desire to raise our children to strive to do their best, not in comparison to others, but for their own sense of accomplishment and satisfaction.

Yes, Nathan and I were honor students. I admit, I was even Valedictorian. But, looking back, much of my schooling revolved around me "working" the system. I simply learned how to "succeed" in public schools and was darn good at it. My actual education, though, in retrospect, was lacking in definite areas. Were it not for my parents and a few key teachers, I might not have learned to *want* to learn, to search out knowledge for its own sake rather than to merely cram it into my head for a term. Were it not for my upbringing, I might easily have been depressed or embarrassed by the "labels" given me by my peers. For our sons, we want better. We don't want them to be defined by grades or by their friends. We don't want them to feel the need to downplay their intellect in exchange for being "cool." We want them to be truly secure in themselves and to have a desire to improve for one's own sake. We want them to be able to recognize success and excellence on their own and to rejoice in it, regardless of what others think. We want them to know that "success" isn't necessarily about being the "best" at something. Success is about achieving what you set out to do. Through homeschooling, we hope to teach them to be proud of their efforts rather than only their results.

This end of the school year picnic with our homeschool group was our first. A tribute to our first "official" completed year of homeschooling. The boys had fun signing each other's shirts and participating in the relay races and water balloon toss. I had fun watching my sons being part of a group while still being completely at ease with who they each are and what they want out of life. If homeschooling continues to bring such benefits, I give it an A+.

my guys

keep moving forward

A+ by Amanda Probst

DARE
TO BE REMARKABLE

no boundaries
100% authentic

insights
MUSINGS
OBSERVATIONS

"Excellence is not a SKILL.
It's an ATTITUDE." —RALPH MARSTON

(#24) EXPERIENCE

Why: To pass along wisdom to others, to remind yourself what your experiences have taught you.

Write about an important experience and what you learned from it. Write about the people in your life who share their wisdom with you. What experiences have changed your life?

★true confessions of a
cheerleader

High school cheerleaders are the epitome of gorgeous and popular with lithe bodies, cute boyfriends, and busy social lives, right? Oh the stereotypes...my story couldn't be further from it!

I was a varsity cheerleader and my experience has no resemblance to the script for a cute Hilary Duff movie. Lithe body? Um, no – maybe when I was five. Cute boyfriends? Not so much. Busy social schedule? I babysat and read books on the weekend. Popular? Well-liked maybe, but certainly not a part of the in crowd. So how could I be a cheerleader? Perhaps I didn't have the typical traits of a cheerleader, but I had unbridled enthusiasm, precision, dedication and SPUNK!

As a grade school cheerleader I had been bossy. My teeny-tiny school allowed everyone to cheer, but I always felt like I

> ❝I was a varsity cheerleader and my experience has no resemblance to the script for a cute Hilary Duff movie.❞

was the only one who *really* cared about it beyond the pom pons and the pleated skirt. In the fall of 1983 I entered high school and headed to the gym to try out for freshman cheerleading. All of a sudden I lost my confidence. The place was filled with girls who apparently had been in gymnastics class since they were three. They could jumper higher than me, and they were thin. I bailed immediately. I knew I didn't stand a chance, so I let go of the dream and left it at that.

In the spring of 1985 I was finishing up my sophomore year, and the cheerleading coach approached me. I had cheered with her daughter in grade school, and she thought that I should give it a go again. I figured if the *coach* thought that I had something to offer then maybe I'd at least try. What did I have to lose? So I did it, hoping to make JV but not really expecting much. I knew that I didn't have the skills

that the other girls had been honing for two years, but I had a big voice, sharp motions, and I loved firing up a crowd. Well, I didn't make the JV squad – **I made Varsity**. This was bigger than I had ever hoped to wish for!

That first year as a cheerleader was anything but easy. The rest of the girls had been working their way up the ranks, and then here I was out of the blue. Some of them weren't particularly nice to me at first.

They felt that I had "stolen" a position on the squad that should've belonged to one of their friends. When it came to choosing uniforms, none of the skirts were large enough for me, so my mom had to make one to fit me. But as the season progressed the other girls figured out why I had made it. I was born to cheer. I was prompt, positive, and passionate. I was enthusiastic, energetic, and extremely dedicated. I was a leader, and I loved to cheer.

The next year as a senior, my peers chose *me* to be the captain. In their eyes I had earned the right and their respect, and I'll never forget that! They put their confidence in me and knew that I'd lead them well.

Years later I became a cheerleading coach and had the opportunity to work with many girls. Quite a few of them had the typical makings of a cheerleader, but through my experience I learned to approach the not so thin and not so popular girls and give them a little push. My instincts were always right. They had what it took.

So thank you, Lenore Lemanski, for encouraging me to try out for cheerleading in the spring of 1985. Being a cheerleader gave me confidence, and I can only hope that I impacted others as you impacted me!

● ● ●

relish the experience

TRUE CONFESSIONS OF A CHEERLEADER by Susan Opel

"There are no failures—just EXPERIENCES
and your REACTIONS to them." —TOM KRAUSE

DENNIS PATTERSON
2ND ROW UP, 2ND FROM RIGHT

My lottery number was 89 so about the time I was to be drafted, I joined so that I could go to flight school. I had already taken the tests and gone thru the selection board for flight school candidates. I scored very high on the entrance exam, a 352. To get in to flight school one only needed 250 on the flight aptitude test to get in. I entered the army in Phoenix at the reception station on 19 January 1971 and was shipped to Fort Polk, Louisiana. My company was D company, 4th Battalion, 1st Basic Combat Training Brigade. I finished in March. Basic was easy and I scored expert in every weapon I fired. It is interesting that almost all the guys who were going to flight school from the civilian world went to Basic at Ft. Polk. Virtually everyone was held over at Polk for about six months as permanent part KP's. That means they were stuck washing dishes for six months. KP means kitchen police. It was horrible. I prayed every day that somehow I would be able to go on to Ft. Wolters Texas and not get held over. Sure enough, my prayers were heard and answered. I went to Ft. Wolters ahead of 450 guys who were stuck at Polk. As a private in the army during basic, I was making $1500 a year. I spent very little of my pay during basic and barely had enough to buy a plane ticket home for two weeks of leave before I went to flight school.

give the reasons

ALMOST DRAFTED by Laura Vanderbeek

(#25) FAMILY

Why: To celebrate the people who have influenced you the most, to remember the family events that have shaped who you are.

Write about your childhood family. Or journal about how your family stays connected to each other. What does your family do for fun?

enjoy each other

YOU. ME. HAPPINESS by Lisa Bearnson

"You don't CHOOSE your family. They are God's GIFT to you, as YOU are to them."
—DESMOND TUTU

journal the everyday

FAMILY COMFORT by Suzy Plantamura, photo by Tara Whitney

IT'S A GIRL

It's all my fault, really. As we were on our way to the hospital for Campbell's induction, I thought, "Campbell's birth story is going to be just like Jason's. I kind of hoped it would be a little different... going into labor on my own or having my water break or something!" It was different alright... We got to the hospital at 8am. We assumed Cam would be born around lunch time since that's how it had gone with Jason. We were so wrong. A couple of hours after the induction started, I felt faint & got really sick. I still felt awful when it came time to push. After pushing for 2.5 hrs, there had been very little progress, so the nurse called Dr. DeRosier in. The Dr. said Campbell had a "brow presentation" (basically coming out face first) and we would have to have a C-section immediately. I was not prepared for that. I had been thinking it was all going to be exactly like it was when I had Jason, but easier. The prospect of a C-section had me completely freaking out. I started sobbing uncontrollably & all I could say was, "Is my baby going to be okay?" to every medical professional I could ask... and there were a lot around to ask. In a matter of minutes, doctors & nurses were all over the room prepping us for surgery. Brian was such a rock. He was worried too, but for my sake he was cool & calm. All I could do was cry, pray & focus on scripture. Focusing on God was the only thing keeping me from going into complete shock. Brian had to stay behind for a few minutes while they took Campbell & me to the OR. He put on scrubs, called our parents to tell them what was going on & prayed before joining us. I could not have made it through the surgery without him being there. The Dr. that delivered Jason, Dr. Davis, assisted with the C-section & that was also comforting. Once we were in the OR, it didn't take long to get Cam out. At 4:45pm Campbell Clemons Burnett was born. She was pink & healthy, thank the Lord. We were beyond relieved. Brian took her to see the family while they finished with me. All I wanted to do was to hold my darling baby girl in my arms & thank the Lord she was finally here safe & sound. We got her around 6:30pm. Our long day was over & our happiness complete.

Feb. 20 2007

SMITTEN

I'll love you forever

she ♥ you

Name: Campbell Clemons Burnett
Date: February 20, 2007 4:45 PM
Weight: 6lbs. 7oz   Length: 19 1/4 in.
Hospital: Brookwood   Doctor: DeRosier
Proud parents: Brian & Katie
Proud brother: Jason
It's a girl!

record sweet moments

IT'S A GIRL by Katie Burnett

"Family MEANS putting your arms AROUND each other and BEING there." —BARBARA BUSH

THOUGHTS ON FAMILY

- Go buy a KITE and fly it as a family! EXPERIMENT with different types of kites and the BEST methods to make your kite FLY.

- Go on a DATE once a week with your SPECIAL someone. It could be a drive in the MOUNTAINS, a movie night or a simple WALK AROUND the block.

- Every night at DINNER, ask your family MEMBERS to share one thing they've learned that DAY. It's insightful conversation because EVERYONE shares what they've LEARNED. Best of all, EACH person has a CHANCE to feel valued.

- The FIRST two words Steve and I TAUGHT our children were "thank" and "you." This has instilled an ATTITUDE of gratitude in them from the TIME they were born. EVEN as teenagers, they're GRATEFUL for even the SMALLEST things.

- Have fun as a FAMILY. Our favorite way to prepare DINNER? We give EACH family member $5 at the grocery STORE and let them buy whatever they want. The CHALLENGE is to keep their purchases a SECRET from everyone else until we REVEAL them that evening. The meal might CONSIST of potato chips, pop, beef jerky AND Chicken-in-a-Biscuit crackers. Definitely not NOURISHING but a whole lot of FUN!

#26 I'M SORRY

Why: To resolve hurtful situations, to apologize to others.

What's forgiveness to you? How do you say "I'm sorry"? When have you extended or received forgiveness?

write the apology

MY APOLOGY by Allison Davis

"I have ALWAYS found that MERCY bears richer FRUITS than strict JUSTICE." —ABRAHAM LINCOLN

I can't help it - I'm my own worst enemy, my own worst critic. But I'm also human - I'm not perfect, I make mistakes, I have my own share of regrets. That's life. I can't help that. The hard part is trying to forgive myself for my mistakes and trying to live without regrets. I tend to dwell on the things I did wrong, and how I could've done things differently. But recently, I've tried to be easier on myself, and try to forgive myself and give myself a break. No one is perfect, and things happen. Accepting them and forgiving myself is just one thing that will help me grow and evolve.

learning to forgive

forgive yourself today

LEARNING TO FORGIVE by Caroline Ikeji

let it go

I FORGIVE MYSELF by Maggie Holmes

...for not being perfect
...for not always keeping a perfectly clean house.
...for not always keeping up on the laundry and ironing.
...for not reading to my children often enough.
...for not playing with my children often enough.
...for sometimes losing my patience too quickly.
At the end of the day I realize that I am doing my best and that's all I can do. They forgive me and they love me no matter what... so I shouldn't be so hard on myself. I forgive ME!

"After all this is OVER, all that will REALLY have mattered is HOW we treated EACH other." —UNKNOWN

#27 FRIENDSHIP

Why: To remember the people who are important to you, to reflect on the lessons you've learned from friends.

Who were your childhood friends? Who are your friends today? How is friendship important in your life?

after being online friends for over a year, we finally met in canada. and it was like we had known each other forever. 10/14/07

scrapbook best friends

WHEN WE MET by Marci Lambert

To our delight, our new pet, Gabby was a big hit to Sean. We brought her home at four months of age and it took a few weeks for Sean to get to know her. They began playing the chase game outside when it was warm out and also with her favorite toy, the stick. While inside, Sean began to hold conversations with her. One conversation went like this after Daphne got sick on the carpet. 'Gabby, Daphne is sick. I am not sick. Are you sick? What do you think, Gabby.' It seemed as though in some way Gabby understood him, or at least she was listening. That is one of the things that we love about her. She plays, listens, and is there for Sean whenever he needs it! Gabby is now seven months, but is already Sean's best buddy!

BEST buddies

play with pets

BEST BUDS by Pam Callaghan

"A BEST friend is someone who MAKES you LAUGH, even when the jokes AREN'T funny."
—KERMIT THE FROG

amber & cara
Nov 2006

friend

share sibling stories

TWINS by Cara Vincens

#28 PAY IT FORWARD

Why: To realize your own blessings, to teach the importance of giving.

How do you give to others? Do you volunteer for an organization, a church or a school? Who do you respect for his or her giving spirit?

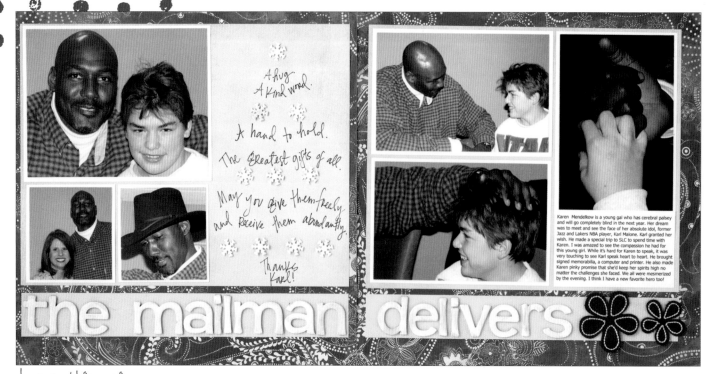

A hug.
A kind word.
A hand to hold.
The greatest gifts of all.
May you give them freely
and receive them abundantly.
Thanks Karl!

Karen Mendelkow is a young gal who has cerebral palsey and will go completely blind in the next year. Her dream was to meet and see the face of her absolute idol, former Jazz and Lakers NBA player, Karl Malone. Karl granted her wish. He made a special trip to SLC to spend time with Karen. I was amazed to see the compassion he had for this young girl. While it's hard for Karen to speak, it was very touching to see Karl speak heart to heart. He brought signed memorabilia, a computer and printer. He also made Karen pinky promise that she'd keep her spirits high no matter the challenges she faced. We all were mesmerized by the evening. I think I have a new favorite hero too!

the mailman delivers

do something nice

THE MAILMAN DELIVERS by Lisa Bearnson

"Give what you HAVE. To someone ELSE, it may be MORE than than YOU'D ever DARE to think."

—HENRY WADSWORTH LONGFELLOW

"To GIVE without any reward
or ANY notice has a SPECIAL quality
of its OWN ." —ANNE MORROW LINDBERGH

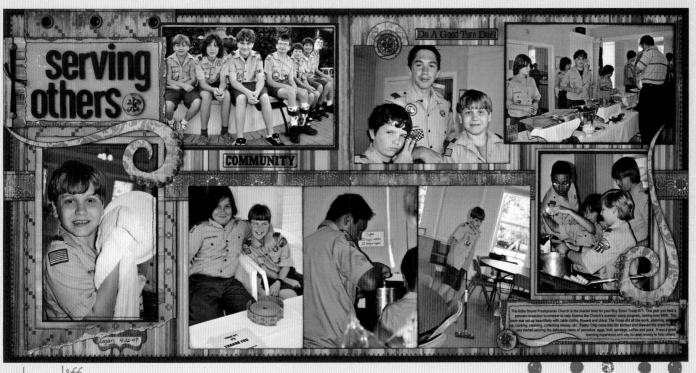

make a difference

SERVING OTHERS by Amy Koeppel

#29 THINK BIG

Why: To make your goals tangible, to provide a place to review your progress

What are your goals and plans at this moment in time? How have your goals changed over the years? Write about a time when you set a goal, went for it and achieved it.

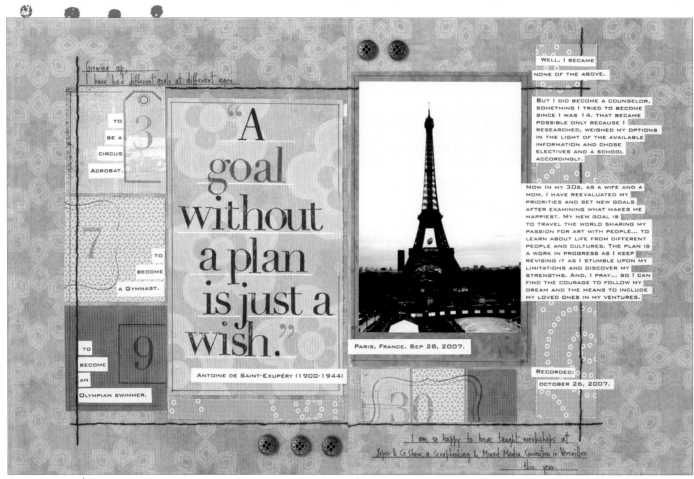

Growing up, I have had different goals at different ages.

TO BE A CIRCUS ACROBAT.

3

TO BECOME A GYMNAST.

7

TO BECOME AN OLYMPIAN SWIMMER.

9

"A goal without a plan is just a wish."

ANTOINE DE SAINT-EXUPÉRY (1900-1944)

PARIS, FRANCE. SEP 28, 2007.

30

WELL, I BECAME NONE OF THE ABOVE.

BUT I DID BECOME A COUNSELOR, SOMETHING I TRIED TO BECOME SINCE I WAS 14. THAT BECAME POSSIBLE ONLY BECAUSE I RESEARCHED, WEIGHED MY OPTIONS IN THE LIGHT OF THE AVAILABLE INFORMATION AND CHOSE ELECTIVES AND A SCHOOL ACCORDINGLY.

NOW IN MY 30S, AS A WIFE AND A MOM, I HAVE REEVALUATED MY PRIORITIES AND SET NEW GOALS AFTER EXAMINING WHAT MAKES ME HAPPIEST. MY NEW GOAL IS TO TRAVEL THE WORLD SHARING MY PASSION FOR ART WITH PEOPLE... TO LEARN ABOUT LIFE FROM DIFFERENT PEOPLE AND CULTURES. THE PLAN IS A WORK IN PROGRESS AS I KEEP REVISING IT AS I STUMBLE UPON MY LIMITATIONS AND DISCOVER MY STRENGTHS. AND, I PRAY... SO I CAN FIND THE COURAGE TO FOLLOW MY DREAM AND THE MEANS TO INCLUDE MY LOVED ONES IN MY VENTURES.

RECORDED: OCTOBER 26, 2007.

I am so happy to have taught workshops at Paper & Co Show, a Scrapbooking & Mixed Media Convention in Versailles this year.

plan your direction

WISH by Mou Saha

"He who FAILS to plan, PLANS to fail." —ANONYMOUS

An adventure is exciting not just while it happens but also in the planning stages. Here, Lisa journals her thoughts about making a big move in her life.

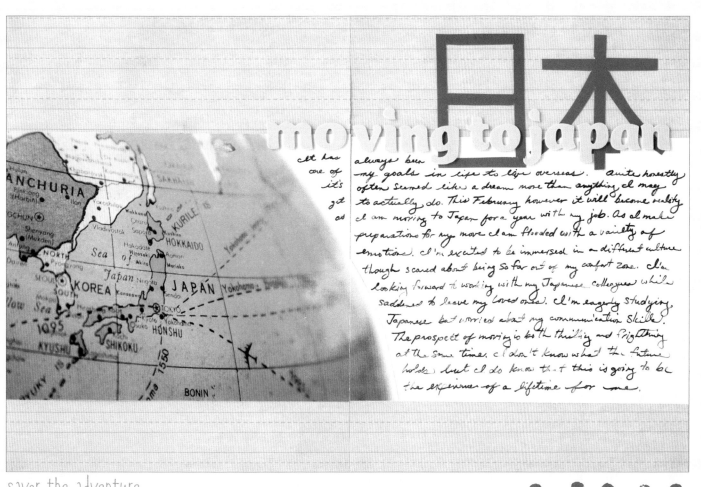

日本

moving to japan

It has always been one of it's goals in life to live overseas. Quite honestly often seemed like a dream more than anything, I may get to actually do. This February however it will become reality as I am moving to Japan for a year with my job. As I make preparations for my move I am flooded with a variety of emotions. I'm excited to be immersed in a different culture though scared about being so far out of my comfort zone. I'm looking forward to working with my Japanese colleagues while saddened to leave my loved ones. I'm eagerly studying Japanese but worried about my communication skills. The prospect of moving is both thrilling and frightening at the same time. I don't know what the future holds but I do know that this is going to be the experience of a lifetime for me.

savor the adventure

MOVING TO JAPAN by Lisa Brown

Make a List

LIFE LISTS by Amanda Probst

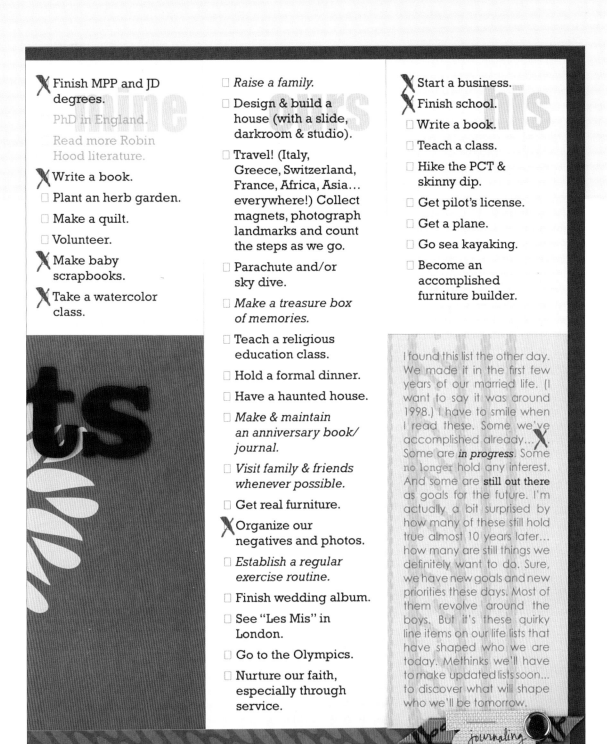

mine

- [X] Finish MPP and JD degrees.

  PhD in England.

  Read more Robin Hood literature.

- [X] Write a book.
- [ ] Plant an herb garden.
- [ ] Make a quilt.
- [ ] Volunteer.
- [X] Make baby scrapbooks.
- [X] Take a watercolor class.

ours

- [ ] *Raise a family.*
- [ ] Design & build a house (with a slide, darkroom & studio).
- [ ] Travel! (Italy, Greece, Switzerland, France, Africa, Asia… everywhere!) Collect magnets, photograph landmarks and count the steps as we go.
- [ ] Parachute and/or sky dive.
- [ ] *Make a treasure box of memories.*
- [ ] Teach a religious education class.
- [ ] Hold a formal dinner.
- [ ] Have a haunted house.
- [ ] *Make & maintain an anniversary book/ journal.*
- [ ] *Visit family & friends whenever possible.*
- [ ] Get real furniture.
- [X] Organize our negatives and photos.
- [ ] *Establish a regular exercise routine.*
- [ ] Finish wedding album.
- [ ] See "Les Mis" in London.
- [ ] Go to the Olympics.
- [ ] Nurture our faith, especially through service.

his

- [X] Start a business.
- [X] Finish school.
- [ ] Write a book.
- [ ] Teach a class.
- [ ] Hike the PCT & skinny dip.
- [ ] Get pilot's license.
- [ ] Get a plane.
- [ ] Go sea kayaking.
- [ ] Become an accomplished furniture builder.

I found this list the other day. We made it in the first few years of our married life. (I want to say it was around 1998.) I have to smile when I read these. Some we've accomplished already... Some are **in progress**. Some no longer hold any interest. And some are **still out there** as goals for the future. I'm actually a bit surprised by how many of these still hold true almost 10 years later... how many are still things we definitely want to do. Sure, we have new goals and new priorities these days. Most of them revolve around the boys. But it's these quirky line items on our life lists that have shaped who we are today. Methinks we'll have to make updated lists soon... to discover what will shape who we'll be tomorrow.

journaling Oct 25, 2007

"Happy people plan ACTIONS, they don't plan RESULTS." —DENNIS WHOLEY

#30 THANK YOU, THANK YOU, THANK YOU

Why: To appreciate the people who've helped you, to count your blessings.

What are you grateful for in your life? How do you personally express thankfulness? How have others expressed thankfulness to you?

count your blessings

WE GIVE THANKS by Stephanie Ackerman

"GRATITUDE is not only the greatest of VIRTUES, but the PARENT of all others." —CICERO

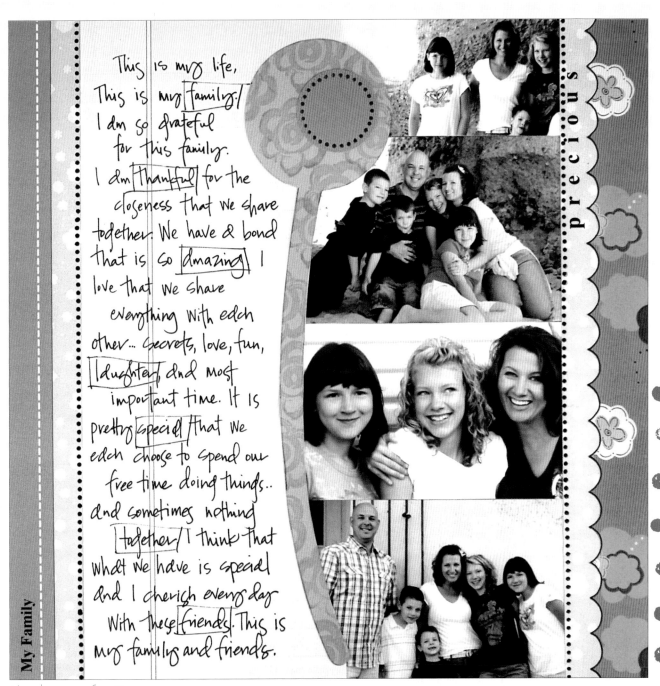

This is my life, This is my family. I am so grateful for this family. I am thankful for the closeness that we share together. We have a bond that is so amazing. I love that we share everything with each other... secrets, love, fun, laughter, and most important time. It is pretty special that we each choose to spend our free time doing things.. and sometimes nothing together. I think that what we have is special and I cherish every day with these friends. This is my family and friends.

My Family

precious

thank your family

MY FAMILY by Jamie Harper

birthday wishes

Continued health, love and happiness. Good friends and good times always. A job I love. To always be creative. To live a life of purpose. May 21st 2007

@ 39

I am blessed   I am blessed   I am blessed   I am blessed   I am blessed   I am blessed   I am blessed

appreciate a birthday

BIRTHDAY WISHES @ 39 by Francine Clouden

" Just TELL yourself, Duckie,
you're really quite LUCKY." —DR. SEUSS

THOUGHTS ON THANKFULNESS

- Be THANKFUL for your family. My husband has a RACE every day with each of our CHILDREN. He asks, "Have I told you TODAY that I LOVE YOU?" The person who can say "I LOVE YOU" first is the winner.

- Be thankful for the JOURNEY. In the summer, my KIDS and I go to the Sundance Resort and climb the MOUNTAIN to Stewart Falls. We ALWAYS have so much FUN along the way—spotting wildlife, finding the best WALKING stick and singing SONGS. When we get to our destination, it's often a LITTLE anti-climactic. WHILE it's BEAUTIFUL, the water is too cold to PLAY in, and it's USUALLY crowded with PEOPLE. This is a good reminder THAT the fun is in the CLIMB, not necessarily in the ARRIVAL.

- Be thankful for your CHILDHOOD. I often sit in front of my childhood HOME and ponder all the wonderful THINGS that happened there. My mind SKIPS from room to room, remembering ALL the HAPPY times we enjoyed within its WALLS. While the home is very small by today's STANDARDS, I thought my FAMILY was rich. Now I KNOW the truth—we were RICH with blessings.

(#31) ON SCHEDULE

Why: To contrast different times of your life, to document your life.

What are your family's routines and schedules? How have your routines and schedules changed over the years? What makes your family's routines unique?

Tuesday Observations

OBSERVATIONS

Tuesday, January 9th - an Ordinary Day. Tuesday Observations. Just another day in the Roger's house. Up at 6:15 to get everyone out the door. Hayden catches the bus @7:25. Madison and I finish to leave before 8. It was snowing on the drive in, lots of blowing (finally). Upon arriving at school, Madison insists on the sensory room. She is adjusting to a new schedule and teacher. I had an ordinary day at work. Ran a few errands at lunch, before picking Madison from school. We headed home at 3:53 pm. A stop along the way showed the storm brewing out over the lake. Hayden and dad had an early game in Negaunee. After they left, Madison and I finished our evening routine and watched as Mya discovered Elmo! Madison finally fell asleep and before the guys returned home from the game (they lost 8-3), I found a little time for me at my scrap desk. The end of our typical day.

record daily events

TUESDAY OBSERVATIONS by Mary Rogers

share bedtime routines

OH IT'S HIPPITY HOP TO BED by Lisa Bearnson

Pages that document your family life—
from what you eat for breakfast, to how
your children greet you when you arrive
home, to your bedtime routines—are an
important look at who you are.

celebrate coming home

A NEW EVENT EVERYDAY by Tracey Odachowski

#32 BE HAPPY

Why: To remember the lighter times, to enjoy the happy moments.

How do you show a sense of humor in your life? What makes you feel happy, content or joyful? What makes you laugh?

make life happy

HILARIOUS by Elizabeth Kartchner

SATURDAY, MARCH 4, 2007 DIDN'T GO EXACTLY LIKE I EXPECTED. IT WAS BRECKEN'S 10TH BIRTHDAY. KADE WAS IN CHARGE OF STRAIGHTENING THE HOUSE FOR BRECKEN'S PARTY. I HAD TO RUN TO THE STORE FOR CUPCAKES AND SUNDAY DINNER INGREDIENTS. I ARRIVED HOME AN HOUR BEFORE THE PARTY, ONLY TO FIND NONE OF THE CHORES HAD BEEN COMPLETED. MAYHEM AND CHAOS WAS HAPPENING IN EVERY ROOM OF THE HOUSE. KADE WAS DRESSED UP LIKE THE BAD GUY ~ BRECKEN, KAITLYN AND LEXI WERE THE GOOD GUYS. SAGE WAS A BEAUTIFUL PRINCESS AND PARIS WAS AN EXOTIC UNICORN.

THE GOOD GUYS WERE FIGHTING THE BAD GUY ~ BOTH WERE TRYING TO CAPTURE THE UNICORN AND THE PRINCESS. RUBBER BANDS WERE BEING SHOT IN EVERY DIRECTION. SCREAMS AND LAUGHTER RESONATED IN EVERY CORNER OF MY HOUSE. AT FIRST I WANTED TO YELL AND SEND EVERYONE HOME. INSTEAD, I SAT ON THE COUCH AND SOAKED UP THIS INCREDIBLE MOMENT. IT HIT ME ~ TOO SOON KADE WILL BE PLAYING "BAD GUY" WITH HIS OWN KIDS AND BRECKEN WILL BE SHOOTING TEXT MESSAGES ~ NOT RUBBER BAND GUNS.

I GRABBED MY CAMERA AND CAPTURED THIS AMAZING MOMENT FOREVER. I FELT PURE JOY, PURE HAPPINESS, PURE CONTENTMENT.

"Always LEAVE enough room in your life to do SOMETHING that MAKES you happy, satisfied or EVEN joyous."

—PAUL HAWKEN

share silly Moments

LOVE, LAUGH, LIVE by Lisa Bearnson

times this year

10975

It's simply amazing the number of times you make me laugh in one day, in one month, in one year. your giggle and sweet smile are explosive, it's such good therapy. i had a small part in giving you life and you return life to me every single day with your sweet laugh. i don't ever want to forget the sweet sound of those ever so ordinary and ever so wonderful laughs. these are truly the moments that make up a lifetime!

laugh

count the reasons

10975 by Laura Kannady

#33 TAKE CARE

Why: To help yourself through a challenging time, to provide medical information to family members.

How do you take care of yourself? What's your health like today? What health challenges do your family members face, and how do you help them?

How could we not?

Elizabeth - 6 years old

It was totally unexpected, totally out of the blue and it has rocked our world. Elizabeth was diagnosed with a seizure disorder and has to be on anti-convulsant meds constantly. We're all adapting and learning something new every single day, but knowing that a seizure could happen at any moment is a bit daunting. She's now developed a bit of an anxiety issue because she's worried about having seizures. But, we'll keep working on it. Look at that face. How could we not?

the light of our lives

journal a challenge

HOW COULD WE NOT? by Stephanie Vetne

"Health is the GREATEST gift." —Buddha

Anna's daughter, Margaret, is a strong little girl who successfully underwent surgery for a rare genetic disorder at just two years old. This page celebrates Margaret's loving, caring, charming personality and Anna's gratitude that her little girl did so well at the hospital.

IT'S JUST EVERY LITTLE THING THAT YOU DO.

my hero

...isses...darling... ...i love you...my sweet pea...my darling... ...i love you to the moon and back...oh so loved...sweetheart... ...hugs and kisses...ing...i love you...

celebrate a great attitude

MY HERO BY ANNE HEYEN

#34 IT'S THE TRUTH

Why: To reflect on what honesty means to you, to impart your values to your family.

What role does honesty play in your life? When is it best to be totally honest? Have you ever been hurt by dishonesty?

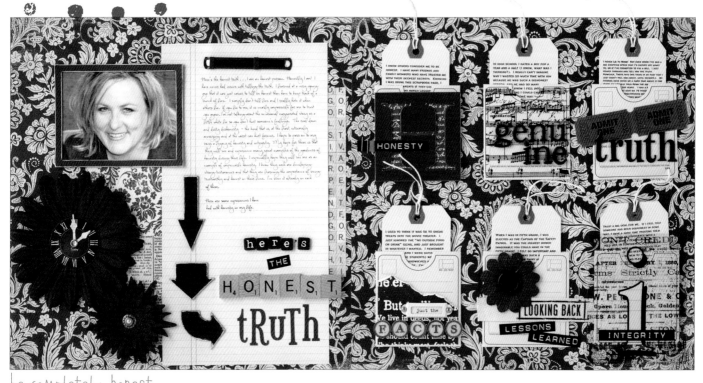

be completely honest

HERE'S THE HONEST TRUTH by Marci Leishman

"HONESTY is the first CHAPTER in the
the book of WISDOM ." —THOMAS JEFFERSON

Do you remember the truth of what it was like to be a kid at Christmas? Share those memories on a page tag like Laura did here.

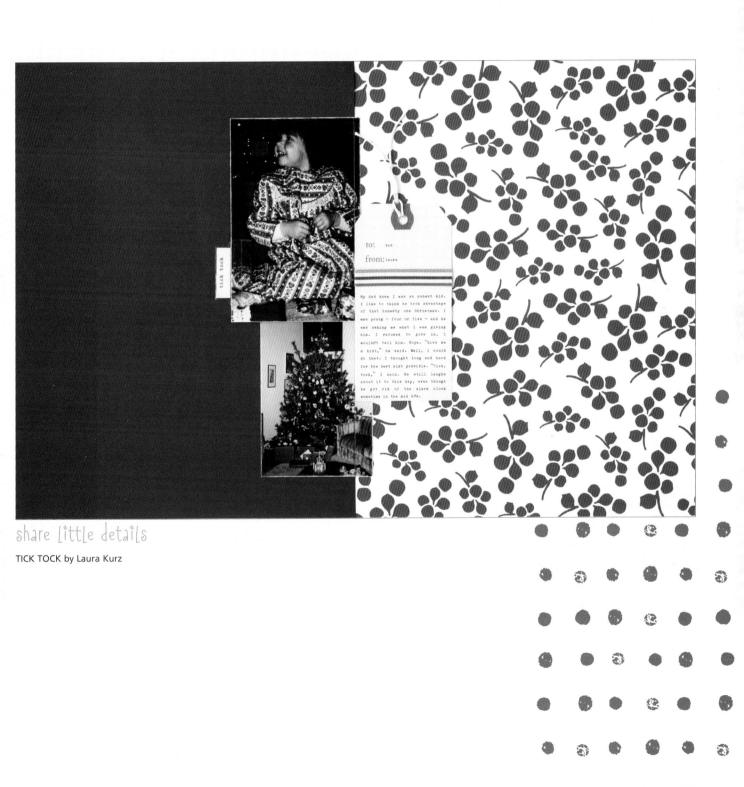

share little details

TICK TOCK by Laura Kurz

The TRUTH, the WHOLE TRUTH, and nothing but the TRUTH.

my-inspiration

examine your truth

THE TRUTH by Amanda Probst

I admit it. I can tell a lie pretty dang well. (Hold the jokes about how appropriate it is that I have a law degree.) Growing up, though I was a model student and citizen, I got away with quite a few lies. Nothing major, honest. But, the fact is that I could tell fibs without breaking a sweat. Exaggeration was a way of life to the point that I truly didn't even notice that I wasn't telling the whole truth. I'm not talking about big, big lies. Heck, they may not even seem like "lies" to some…promising one thing and not doing it or stating unequivocally that something "always" happened. They certainly didn't seem all that wrong to me…just little things in daily life that all added up to a habit. A habit where honesty's definition was stretched and telling half-truths didn't faze me.

And then I met Nathan. He is one of the most honest people I've ever known. He tells the truth almost to a fault. (Let's just say it's taken some considerable coaching during our marriage to get him to either not answer the "how does this look?" questions or to say something nice…and I've learned it's generally better to just not ask.) Talking with him and living with him has challenged me to re-examine how I approach the truth. Add parenting (and some very literal boys) to the mix, and I've truly learned the importance of meaning what you say and saying what you mean. I want my boys to follow in their father's footsteps and be men of integrity. I want them to continue knowing that lying will get them in more trouble than telling the truth. I want them to understand the importance of promises and the power of their words. I work now to choose my own words with more care and struggle to impart this to my boys. I do my best to only make threats I intend to carry through with and promises I can keep…and, truthfully, this still takes me some mental effort. But it's important. So I'll keep trying. Honest.

(#35) BE KIND

Why: To think about what kindness means to you, to share stories about kindness in action.

How has an act of kindness (given or received) had an impact on your life? What's your definition of kindness? Why do you think it's important to be kind?

you earned this

It was at your 11th birthday party. You and your friends were sitting around the table, eating breakfast. Your family was in the kitchen, making breakfast. You were all talking, like preteens do. One of your friends polled the group. "Raise your hand if you hate your brother." All but two hands shot up. Shelby is an only child. You looked straight at your brother and smiled. Right there, you won his heart forever babe.

be an example

YOU EARNED THIS by Emily Pitts

When you turned 18 months old you started going to Nursery in church for two hours every Sunday. This was a big deal for both you and me. We spent every day together, and I had never taken you to a day care center, or any place where you were surrounded by other kids and left without me. Dad and I like to go into the Nursery room with you when we drop you off and hang out until you are settled in and happily playing with some plastic blocks or the kitchen set. The first thing you always go for in Nursery is your "baby." It is the only baby doll in the room, and it seems like everyone knows that it is "Lia's baby." You tuck her under your arm and she happily accompanies you as you play with the other toys and kids.

One Sunday we took you to Nursery before the toys were taken out of the cupboard. We urged you to stand by the cupboard and wait for the Nursery leader to give you your doll, which you did, albeit a bit nervously. By the time the leader arrived to unlock the cupboard, you had been joined by a few other kids waiting for the toys. She unlocked the door and pulled out your baby. You took a little step forward and started to reach out for it. However, the Nursery leader handed your baby to the girl standing next to you. The little girl was delighted. You tuned to her and made a feeble, pleading "please" sign. She ignored you.

In my head I was urging you to just reach out and take it from her. I didn't want you to be the one in Nursery who has her toys stolen away all the time. No, I wanted you to be strong, assertive, a leader.

Then you reached out and did it, as if you could hear what I was silently urging you to do. You stole the doll right out of the girl's hands. Before you even realized what you had done, the girl snatched the doll right back from you. You spun around and looked at Dad and me with these round, pleading eyes. You didn't know what to do. That was your baby and someone else had it. Before I could react the Nursery leader distracted you with another toy, and you went on your merry way.

your tender heart

I will admit that looking back I am quite ashamed that I rejoiced in your bad behavior. You didn't know better, you weren't even two! But I, I do know better. I know that sometimes it seems like we have to take what want in this world, whether it is ours or not. Sometimes sacrifices or acts of kindness go unnoticed and unrewarded. Sometimes bad behavior goes by unnoticed or is even applauded. The world has a way of hardening people's hearts. But you can't let it harden you. The world may tell you that you must please yourself first. But I will tell you that the only way to truly be happy is through kindness and service to others. I hope I can teach you that, even though sometimes I feel like the world has hardened me. Keep your tender heart. Serve others. Speak kind words. That is where you will find your joy.

hEaRt

follow your heart

YOUR TENDER HEART by Jill Hornby

"No act of kindness, no matter how small is ever wasted." --Aesop

A prayer for Nichole...

I went to my doctor's appointment in preparation for eye surgery. The technician was putting eye drops in my eyes to dilate them when she commented how smart I was to have no make-up on. I simply told her I had no make-up on because I had been up since 2:00 am that morning. She asked why I had been up that long.

I explained that my daughter had been in the emergency room after just being released from a 7 day hospital stay. She went in the hospital for an out-patient procedure and ended up in the hospital for a week. Now, we were back again because my daughter was in severe pain.

The technician asked my daughter's name and assured me that she would pray for Nichole that evening. I learned that the technician's name was Kim. We were complete strangers but I will always be grateful to her for the small act of kindness that had such a reassuring comfort in our lives. Thank you Kim!

October 2007

Kindness

plant seeds of kindness

KINDNESS by Pam Taylor

#36 WRITE HOW YOU FEEL

Why: To share how you tell a story, to give historical perspective on how we communicate today.

What's your preferred method of communication? How do you stay in touch with family and friends? Tell a story about a conversation that made you laugh or that impacted your life.

We all couldn't help but laugh at Keane, who decided to wait about an hour before the ceremony to write his toast. I think Kathy had written her toast days before, even typing it up nicely. Keane, on the other hand, was using paper stolen from his hotel room. I guess his procrastination could also be seen as spontaneity... his speech was funny, heartfelt, and memorable. Totally one hundred percent Keane.

a little procrastination

write it out

A LITTLE PROCRASTINATION by Kelly Purkey

Conversations that you have with others can be a powerful way to journal about your thoughts, beliefs, hopes and dreams. Take a moment and write down a conversation that would help someone you know.

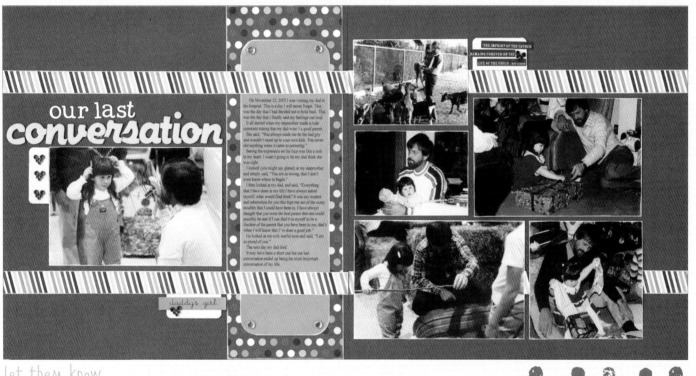

let them know

OUR LAST CONVERSATION by Allison Davis

essentia

There's no combination of words I could put on the back of a postcard.

Our dreams, and they are made out of real things

Love is the answer, At least for most of the questions in my heart

It's not always easy and Sometimes life can be deceiving

keep it real

ESSENTIALS by Jackie Stringham

No song that I could sing, but I can try for your heart

Like a, shoebox of photographs With sepiatone lovin'

Like why are we here? And where do we go? And how come it's so hard?

I'll tell you one thing it's always better when we're together

"One who CARES is one who listens."

—ANONYMOUS

Today is my Anniversary -- seven years. But I feel cheated every time that I say seven years because we were together LONG before we got married. I mean almost 18 years together (including our 7 married years). But I'll be all grown up about it and go by the legal date (even if I do still feel cheated).

It's nice thinking back to what I was doing about this time (8:41) seven years ago. I had already said my vows (during which I swayed almost the entire time). We had survived the drive to the reception in our vintage Rolls Royce by a woman who was clearly impaired and didn't know how to drive a normal car let alone an antique. I had finally escaped my photographer who insisted on pulling me away during dinner when all that I wanted to do was eat-- but we did get some nice shots outside. The rain had finally stopped and the evening was beautiful. I was trying my hardest to get to the ladies room while getting cornered by every guest who wanted to personally congratulate me (the nerve of them). And I was over the moon happy and in love because it was the day I had dreamed about and I was going to be married to my perfect guy – forever.

You know the great thing is that I still dig that guy today – something awful. And I wouldn't change where I am in my life right now for anything. I am one seriously lucky gal. And I have some really great memories!

capture a moment

REWIND by Marla Kress

A happy page deserves bright happy colors, fun fonts and playful lines. As you scrapbook, remember that your entire page is communicating the message you want to share with others.

The first time I met Steve I thought "Wow - this is a guy who really knows how to have

fun

Seventeen years later and nothing has changed! People want to be around Steve because he is

happy

and can always bring a

smile

to your face.

He knows how to

PLAY

hard and laugh about any situation.

He will be known for generations

to come for his delightful personality

feel comfortable and loved.

and the ability to make others

HURRAY for steve!

Photos taken in Orlando, Florida April 2007

appreciate loved ones

HURRAY FOR STEVE by Lisa Bearnson

THINGS I LOVE *about you*

On this **Valentines Day** I am amazed that I still feel such powerful sparks between us.

People say all of the time that the magic fades, but **cupid's arrow** hit almost 12 years ago and I still get thousands of butterflies when I am around you. There are so many things that I love about you, and although I am not the greatest at telling you I want you to know **how I feel.**

I love the way I catch you looking at me, it makes me melt to feel the love from you.
I love the time you invest in our family. There are so many things to accomplish in a day and yet our family time is number one to you.
I love the way you **take my hand** or touch the small of my back.
I love catching you belting out a song.
I love when I come home and you already have dinner made.
I love that you will watch girly movies just to be with me.
I love watching your enthusiasm as you create art from a piece of wood.
I love to see your competitive side when you play a pick up game of basketball.
I love the way you love me. We have always been best friends, and maybe that is why the **sparks still fly. I love you.**

share your feelings

THINGS I LOVE ABOUT YOU by Jamie Harper

" Love is a GIFT . Don't ask for the RECEIPT."

—KERMIT THE FROG

THOUGHTS ON LOVE

Scrapbooking is a WONDERFUL way to preserve your family memories, but it's also a wonderful place to SHOW people in your life JUST how much you love them. Think about creating LAYOUTS centered around the FOLLOWING topics:

- A TIME when you anticipated meeting SOMEONE special or spending time with YOUR loved ones during a birthday PARTY or holiday event.

- How you FEEL when you COME home from a hard DAY at work and find your family waiting to greet YOU and welcome you home.

- EXAMPLES of times WHEN your family cheered you up, made you feel happy or brought a smile to YOUR face.

- Stories about the LITTLE things you do to show that you care or stories about how people have helped take CARE of you during a TOUGH patch or illness.

- A conversation you had with SOMEONE that made you really reflect on your LIFE, that helped you make a BIG decision, or that PUT you on a different life path.

IT'S A MISTAKE

Why: To learn from mistakes, to offer reassurance that we're all human.

Write about a mistake you've made, big or small. What did you learn from it? What would you like others to learn from it?

The biggest mistake I made in college was losing touch with these girls, Jen, Jenny, Sara and Nikki. I could use the excuse that life got in the way. But all that really is is an excuse, I should have tried harder. When we get together now, 10 years later, it's like nothing has ever changed. I won't forget in the decades to come how much you girls meant to me and how much you still mean to me.

find the positive

HIGH SCHOOL FRIENDS by Laura Kurz

"Mistakes are the PORTALS of discovery."

–JAMES JOYCE

Here, Marci packs a ton of information on a two page spread. Each of the numbers on her layout represents a lesson that she's learned.

reflect on lessons

LESSONS LEARNED by Marci Leishman

(#39) ENJOY LIFE

Why: To show a lighter side of yourself, to remember to make time to have fun.

Describe how you play . . . what do you enjoy doing just for the sheer joy of it? What types of songs make you want to dance? Perhaps you love art or enjoy a sport or love to craft—write about it!

JULY 2007

It was the 5th straight day of rain in early July, and you were going stir-crazy. So when you begged to go outside and play in the rain, how could I say no? Your exuberance made it a treat for you AND me!

learn to laugh

100% CHANCE OF RAIN by Linda Rodriguez

Create a layout about the things you love to do!
Imagine the connection a family member could feel by
picking up one of your favorite books and reading it.

There's nothing better than crawling in my pjs and cuddling up with a good book. I've been in the middle of daring sword fights, exotic deserted islands and castles fit only for a Queen. When I'm in the middle of a good book, I can't quit thinking about it throughout the day. The anticipation of how the story will end about kills me! I love it!

read a book

I LOVE BOOKS by Lisa Bearnson

SUN | MON | TUE | WED | THUR | FRI | SAT

365 days a year I cherish you.
You are my world you
are my everything. ♥

simply beautiful.

Romance.

cherish

family forever and
always.
2007 photos.

Fun

keep an album

CHERISH ALBUM by Jamie Harper

"Today was GOOD. Today was FUN.
TOMORROW is another one!" —DR. SEUSS

SUN	MON	TUE	WED	THUR	FRI	SAT

I love having our family photos all in one place so I can have it on my desk to look at everyday while you are at school.
I miss you like crazy all day and count the hours until you are home again. Who knew motherhood would feel this way?

...we are a happy family... sometimes

FAMILY

Summer vacation is my favorite. While the other mom's are doing the happy dance that school is back in session after 3 long months I am crying for days before just knowing that you will soon be gone all day. I love our family, I love our relationship, I love the fun that we have together, and I love life with each of you in it. I cherish our family and our time together. You are each so special to me in your own way and I love how

SUNDAY ALL THROUGH THE YEAR HAPPY TIMES FAMILY TIMES BEDTIMES GOOD FOOD

you are each so different. You are my everything. ♥

Family (fe-milî), pA. ME. [ad. L. familia The body of persons who live in on house or under one head, including parents, children, servants, etc. b. the group consisting of parents and their children, whether living together or not; in wider sense, all those who are easily connected by blood or affinity 1867. b. A person's children regarded collectively 1732.

Family

A LOT OF ENERGY IS COMING FROM

Fun

(#40) BE PATIENT

Why: To provide hope to others that waiting is worth it, to share your thoughts on a core value.

When in your life have you had to be patient? When has persistence paid off for you? When has the anticipation driven you crazy?

month: June

			1	2	3
☆	☆	☆			
4	5	6	7	8	9
10	11	⑫	13	14	15
16	17	18	19	20	21
22	23	24	25	26	27
28	29	30	31	☆	☆

Baby Kennedy I have been waiting for you for such a long time. Sure the kids have other cousins, but I have been waiting for a niece or nephew from my sisters. I have been waiting for 5 years for you. There is something very special about my baby sister, and with you, comes that same special feeling. If this is what being an Aunt feels like, then I can't wait to be a Grandma.

Shy baby.

anticipate the arrival

WAITING by Jamie Harper

"ALL human WISDOM is summed up in TWO words: wait and HOPE." —ALEXANDRE DUMAS, PÈRE

Dream It. Believe It. Achieve It... this motto has been painted on the walls of her schools and etched on the fibers of her heart. And if you were to read between the lines of her resume, you would see the theme repeated over and over: teacher, dean, AP, principal and most recently... Dr. and new school principal. In the short span of a few years, this amazing woman has achieved a doctorate degree and managed to open a brand new middle school. It has not come without sacrifices. It has not come without struggle

ACHIEVE IT

and heartache. But she has the largest cheering section in the state of Nevada – the famLea – and an inspiring drive to succeed and achieve. Thanks, Dr. Lea, for teaching us to Dream It. Believe It. Achieve It. Your example has certainly inspired us to achieve our own dreams.

Joy Lea and the brand new Faiss MS August 2007

never give up
ACHIEVE IT by Jaime Lynne Lea Woodmansee

#41 RESPECT

Why: To remember to respect differences, to pass along a core value.

What does respect mean to you? Who do you respect and for what reasons? Do you believe respect is a given, or do you believe it should be earned?

All she needs is a golden lasso and Liz is ready to take on the world. To me, she is Wonder Woman. Liz represents all that I wish I could be. When I was moving to Chicago, she helped me get an interview at the old Career Builder.com office she used to work in. During the interview, as soon as anyone heard that I knew Liz they immediately started gushing about what an amazing person she is. In this huge company Liz and her talents were famous. (After all, she did get hired on-the-spot during her interview there!) Now after taking night classes to complete her MBA this year, she is quickly climbing her way to the top of the business world. I have such respect for a woman who can earn success in business and do it with a sense of humor and positive attitude like Liz has. She makes me laugh, spends the day scrapbooking with me, and is always up for meeting me for guacamole. There is nothing this woman can't do. Maybe she doesn't need the golden lasso after all.

acknowledge a friend's strengths

WONDER WOMAN by Kelly Purkey

"Respect YOURSELF and others WILL respect you." —CONFUCIUS

document family characteristics

CHERISH RESPECT by Marci Leishman

practice being kind

RESPECT by Maggie Holmes

#42 SHHH—IT'S A SECRET!

Why: To reveal a part of your personality that others may not have seen; to share funny, silly things that will make others laugh.

What secrets do you have that you're willing to share? Tell a story about a time when you spilled a secret or when you were part of a secret (maybe planning a surprise party or sharing fun gifts with secret sisters). What's the best part of having a secret?

share something silly

CAN YOU KEEP A SECRET? by Kelly Purkey

"Secrets are things we GIVE to OTHERS to keep for us." —ELBERT HUBBARD

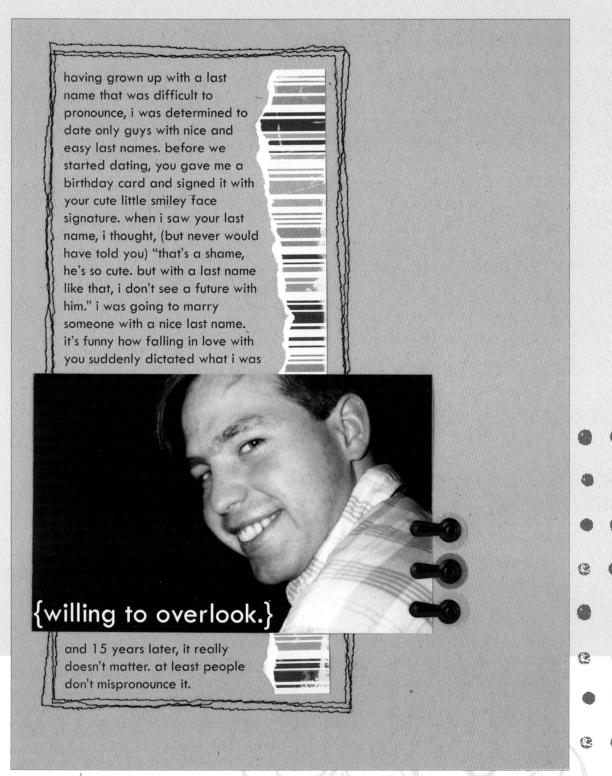

having grown up with a last name that was difficult to pronounce, i was determined to date only guys with nice and easy last names. before we started dating, you gave me a birthday card and signed it with your cute little smiley face signature. when i saw your last name, i thought, (but never would have told you) "that's a shame, he's so cute. but with a last name like that, i don't see a future with him." i was going to marry someone with a nice last name. it's funny how falling in love with you suddenly dictated what i was

{willing to overlook.}

and 15 years later, it really doesn't matter. at least people don't mispronounce it.

tell it today

WILLING TO OVERLOOK by Emily Pitts

remember early moments

NO MORE SECRETS by Jill Hornby

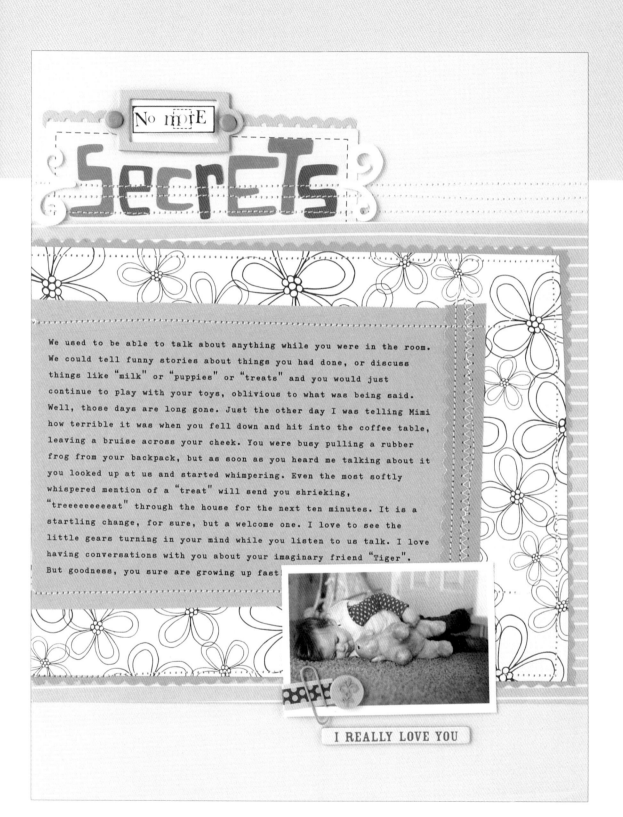

No morE

SECRETS

We used to be able to talk about anything while you were in the room. We could tell funny stories about things you had done, or discuss things like "milk" or "puppies" or "treats" and you would just continue to play with your toys, oblivious to what was being said. Well, those days are long gone. Just the other day I was telling Mimi how terrible it was when you fell down and hit into the coffee table, leaving a bruise across your cheek. You were busy pulling a rubber frog from your backpack, but as soon as you heard me talking about it you looked up at us and started whimpering. Even the most softly whispered mention of a "treat" will send you shrieking, "treeeeeeeeeeat" through the house for the next ten minutes. It is a startling change, for sure, but a welcome one. I love to see the little gears turning in your mind while you listen to us talk. I love having conversations with you about your imaginary friend "Tiger". But goodness, you sure are growing up fast!

I REALLY LOVE YOU

#43 SILENCE IS NOURISHING

Why: To gather your thoughts and feeling, to share your beliefs.

How many different types of silence can you describe? How does silence nourish you? Where do you find peace and quiet?

I KNOW IT SOUNDS CRAZY, BUT ONE OF MY FAVORITE PLACES TO MEDITATE IS AT THE CEMETERY. I LOVE TO SIT BY AN ANCESTOR'S GRAVE AND THINK ABOUT THE LIFE THEY LED – THE JOYS, SORROWS, AND TRIALS THEY EXPERIENCED. THE SILENCE IS TRANQUIL; THE THOUGHTS ARE NOURISHING. I ALWAYS LEAVE BUOYED UP AND READY TO TACKLE THE WORLD. I FEEL STRENGTH IN KNOWING FAMILY MEMBERS THAT HAVE GONE BEFORE ME ARE CHEERING FOR ME AND WANT ME AND MY FAMILY TO SUCCEED.

Silence is NOURISHING

take time out

SILENCE by Lisa Bearnson

IKEA duvet + flannel Target snowflake sheets + four pillows = my sanctuary.

As a kid, I remember running to my bedroom, jumping into bed, and pulling the covers over my head... thinking nobody could see me and bother me. Maybe I still believe that today. My bed is still my time out sanctuary. It s the place I always run to for some peace and quiet. When I m having a bad day and just want to tune everything out, I grab a book and head to bed. No matter how awful things are, I can climb into bed and calm down. Even if I m fully dressed, I can just burrow down inside and be relaxed. The soft blankets and pillows wrap me up in a big hug.

And I m never too old for that.

explain the whys

UNDER THE COVERS by Kelly Purkey

"Silence is the SLEEP that nourishes WISDOM."

—SIR FRANCIS BACON

display your comforts

MY SAFE PLACE by Glenda Tkalac

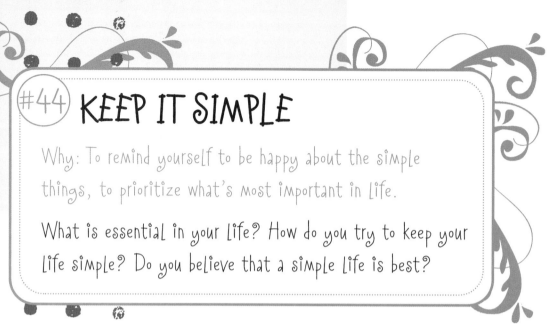

#44 KEEP IT SIMPLE

Why: To remind yourself to be happy about the simple things, to prioritize what's most important in life.

What is essential in your life? How do you try to keep your life simple? Do you believe that a simple life is best?

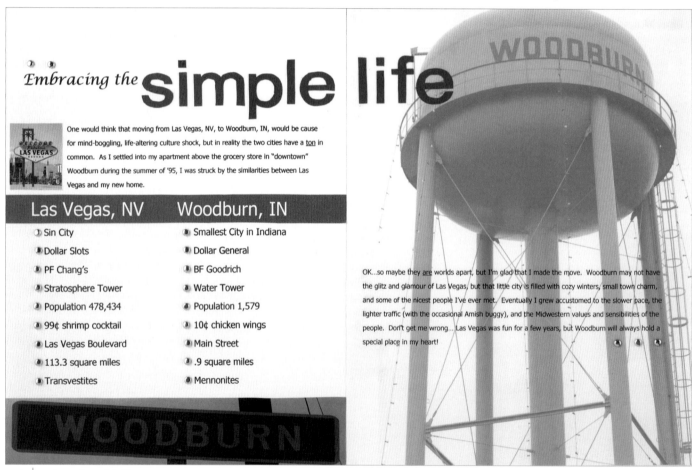

Embracing the simple life

One would think that moving from Las Vegas, NV, to Woodburn, IN, would be cause for mind-boggling, life-altering culture shock, but in reality the two cities have a <u>ton</u> in common. As I settled into my apartment above the grocery store in "downtown" Woodburn during the summer of '95, I was struck by the similarities between Las Vegas and my new home.

Las Vegas, NV	Woodburn, IN
Sin City	Smallest City in Indiana
Dollar Slots	Dollar General
PF Chang's	BF Goodrich
Stratosphere Tower	Water Tower
Population 478,434	Population 1,579
99¢ shrimp cocktail	10¢ chicken wings
Las Vegas Boulevard	Main Street
113.3 square miles	.9 square miles
Transvestites	Mennonites

OK...so maybe they <u>are</u> worlds apart, but I'm glad that I made the move. Woodburn may not have the glitz and glamour of Las Vegas, but that little city is filled with cozy winters, small town charm, and some of the nicest people I've ever met. Eventually I grew accustomed to the slower pace, the lighter traffic (with the occasional Amish buggy), and the Midwestern values and sensibilities of the people. Don't get me wrong... Las Vegas was fun for a few years, but Woodburn will always hold a special place in my heart!

WOODBURN

celebrate simplicity

EMBRACE THE SIMPLE LIFE by Susan Opel

"SOMETIMES the questions are COMPLICATED and the ANSWERS are simple." —DR. SEUSS

Struggling to put your feelings into words?
A favorite quote can help put your thoughts into
perspective (but journal with your own words
sometimes, too!)

CLOUDS

I think the world really boils down to two types of people - those who see shapes in cloud formations, and those who just see clouds.

~Danzae Pace

choose to imagine

CLOUDS by Summer Fullerton

showcase the everyday

GIRL TALK by Jackie Stringham

It happens at least once a day.

It makes me smile and sometimes cry.

It can be silly and serious.

It happens by phone, email, letter and together

It can last hours or minutes.

Mostly it is her, but sometimes it is them.

It is us.

"Simplicity is the ULTIMATE sophistication."

—LEONARDO DA VINCI

#45 TREASURE CHEST

Why: To share pictures and stories of family heirlooms, to create a visual accounting of precious items.

What are your valued possessions? Where did you get them, and why are they special to you? Will you pass them along to a family member one day?

THESE ARE MY TREASURES

These paintings are one of my greatest treasures. They represent my most incredible blessings—four beautiful children. They were painted by a dear friend and depict a time in my children's lives that I want to remember forever.

Thank goodness for Steven Kade Bearnson. He's honorable, responsible, friendly and courteous. So glad he's the oldest. What a great example for his siblings to follow.

Thank goodness for Collin Downs Bearnson. He's sensitive, honest, unselfish and our little peacemaker. He's also kind to everyone.

Thank goodness for Brecken Elizabeth Bearnson. She's smart, helpful and has a huge heart. She fills our home with beautiful music—whether it's singing or playing the piano.

Thank goodness for Sage Adeline Bearnson. She's compassionate, sweet and a little show off—she makes us laugh! Her continual "I Love You" notes make our day.

I am truly blessed and I can't ask for anything more.

share your treasures

THESE ARE MY TREASURES by Lisa Bearnson

"A BOX without hinges, key or LID, yet GOLDEN treasure INSIDE is hid." –J. R. R. TOLKIEN

Love, love, love this! This is the first picture/note you tried to write to me all on your own... It says "LO BRETT" with seashells around it, which you read to me as "LOVE BRETT". ♥ you too buddy! so much.

sweet ♥
REMEMBER
Aug. 16/07

'LOVE BRETT'

you

TO LIVE WITHOUT LOVE IS TO NOT REALLY LIVE

safeguard a note

LOVE BRETT by Sarah Joseph

#46 WORKING FOR A LIVING

Why: To share your work ethic, to document your career path.

What type of work do you currently do? What kind of work have you done in the past? If you could do any kind of work, what would it be?

You did it! You've become a licensed Real Estate Appraiser! Taking a new career path has been quite a journey, as anyone would expect. First, there were 6 months of class training to become qualified for an internship. During that time we were expecting our first baby! Matt, who was also perusing the same new career, got you connected with an Appraisal business opening a second branch. They took you on and you spent your first part as an Intern under them. There was a nationwide boom in realty at that time, which made it an incredibly demanding market to begin a new career in. Adding to that, you had also become a new father! It was quite a rollercoaster time in our lives. After 1½ years interning, Matt, connected you again; he introduced you to the company he was working for. They wanted to bring you on board, but we wondered whether or not you should leave the company which gave you your beginning. After a lot of prayer, you were lead to join Empire Appraisals. It was another 6 months before your 2-year internship was fulfilled. You turned in all the necessary paperwork: log of 2500 hours experience, applications, identifications, background check, etc. Despite a lot of anxiety, you passed the intense state exam on your fist try, which took many of your colleagues 2-3 attempts. I prayed the whole time during your test! When you called me with the victorious news, I was so proud of you! So much relief and thankfulness fell upon us. Appraising homes requires a lot of driving across all sorts of terrain. A brand new truck is an exciting commodity we are able to provide for you. And just like your official Appraisal license, THIS license has a lot of meaning, too. Double meaning actually! You are an "Appraiser", and you are "A Praiser" (drummer on the church worship team). CONGRATS ON BECOMING LICENSED, JERRY!

Jerry P. LaMontagne

Real Estate Appraiser

Licensed: September 24, 2004

explore new opportunities

LICENSED by Leah LaMontagne

"There is no SUBSTITUTE for hard work . . . GENIUS is ONE percent inspiration and NINETY-NINE percent perspiration."

—THOMAS ALVA EDISON

I thought I was so over the Courier. But a year after walking away, I realize that I do really miss it. I miss writing, I miss coming up with stories, I miss knowing everything that goes on on campus. I miss going to JACC, hanging out there, and the thrill of competition and earning an award. I miss the staffers and all their quirks, and ruling the paper with Kate. I miss the photogs and listening to their Canon vs. Nikon debate all day long. I miss the Mako Bowl & Zankou food runs, and John's crazy coffee beans.

miss this

Caroline Ikeji
Pasadena City College
Editor
293-1227

I even miss B yelling at us and seeing all the red marks on an edited copy. All I know is that my time on staff was so worthwhile and that I am so thankful for the experience. It's part of me.

scrapbook career experiences

MISS THIS by Caroline Ikeji

#47 FAMILY TRADITIONS

Why: To pass along the traditions that make your family special, to celebrate special moments.

What are your most cherished family traditions for celebrating anniversaries, birthdays, holidays and more? What family traditions are unique to your culture or your family?

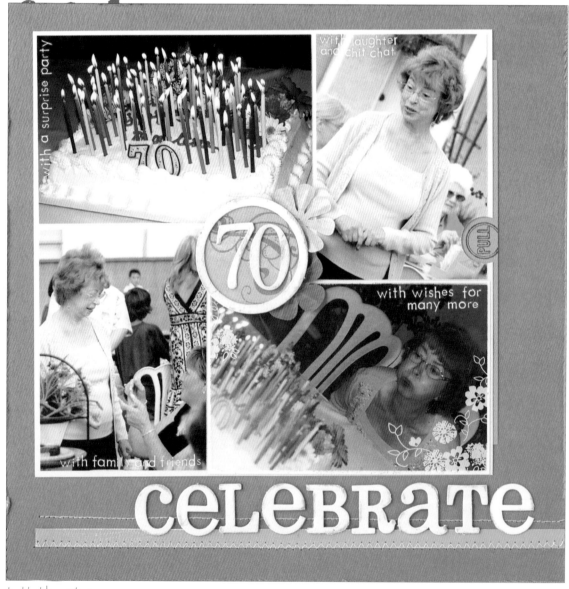

tell the story

CELEBRATE by Denise Pauley

Holiday traditions are special. They give us something to look forward to each year and help define who we are as a family.

Grandma's

Christmas

Tradition

The Downs family always has a big Christmas party just before Christmas. We open presents, eat a huge meal and enjoy a talent show put on by the kids. However, two events we look forward to the most are thanks to Grandma Downs. Every year she lovingly makes or buys an ornament for each grandchild. The kids will all have quite an ornament collection when they leave home. She also reads a special holiday story then randomly picks a grandchild to receive the book.

Everyone looks forward to Grandma's traditions. They will be loved and cherished for generations to come.

enjoy the moments

CHRISTMAS TRADITIONS by Lisa Bearnson

"TRADITION: a clock that TELLS us what TIME it is." —ELBERT HUBBARD

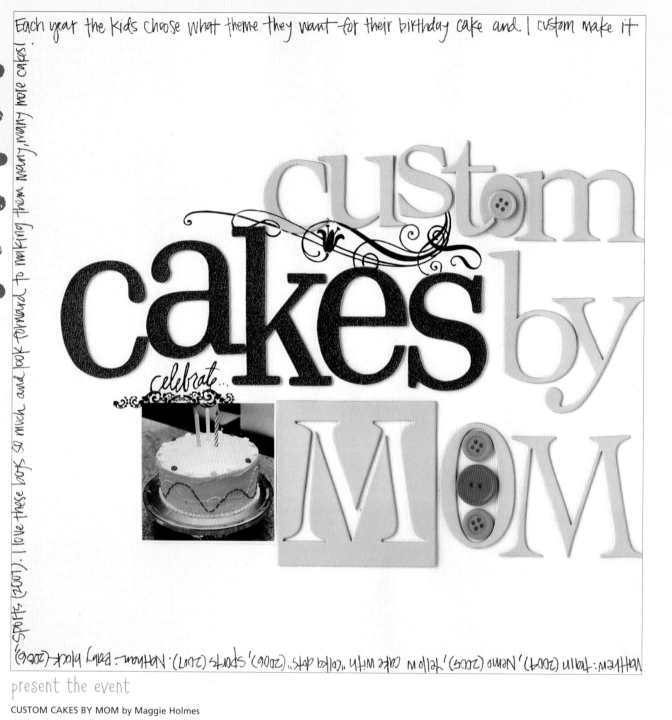

Each year the kids choose what theme they want for their birthday cake and I custom make it

"Sports (2007). I love these boys so much and look forward to making them many, many more cakes!

Matthew: Train (2004), Nemo (2005), yellow cake with "polka dots" (2006), sports (2007). Nathan: yellow cake - baby block (2006)

present the event

CUSTOM CAKES BY MOM by Maggie Holmes

just for them. It is one of my favorite traditions that we have! I love to make the cakes and they love that they get a special cake made just for them by their mom. We have had so many fun cakes

our birthday tradition

enjoy

over the years: Tyler: giraffe (2002), sports (2003), train (2004), spiderman (2005), Cars Movie (2006), spiderman (2007).

"Start a new TRADITION today!" —ELBERT HUBBARD

(#48) A FEW OF MY FAVORITE THINGS

Why: To paint a picture of who you really are, to share how you change over the years.

What are your favorites? How have your favorites changed over the years? Why do you love the things you do?

show your favorites

LUCKY by Lisa Bearnson

"Raindrops on ROSES and WHISKERS on kittens . . ."

—FROM *THE SOUND OF MUSIC*

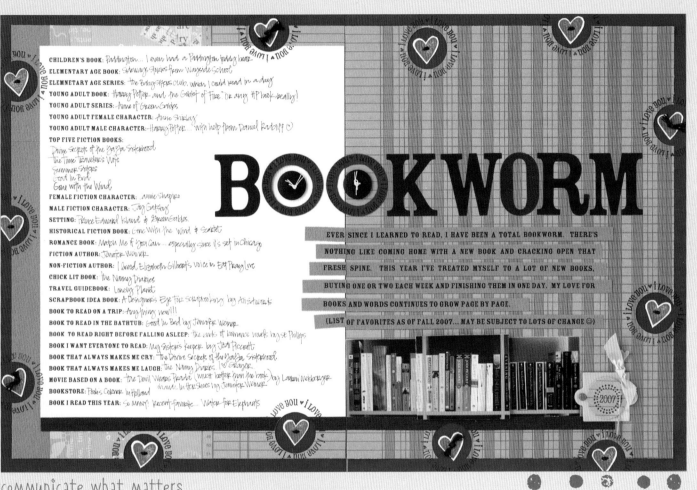

communicate what matters

BOOKWORM by Kelly Purkey

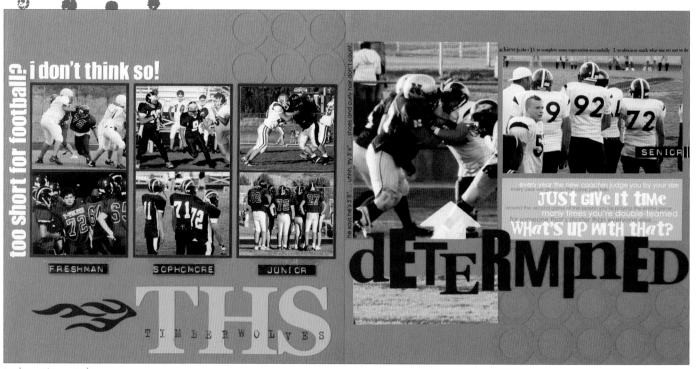

#49 JUST SAY YES!

Why: To celebrate the times when you took a risk, to recognize all of the positives in your life.

When do you say yes? Do you ever say yes when you really mean no? What would you like to say yes to in your life? Are there any "yes" answers you regret?

take the risk

DETERMINED by Kerri Bradford

"I MEANT what I said, and I SAID what I meant."

—DR. SEUSS

It's so easy to say no, but I think it's also important to say yes whenever we can! Say yes to something today!

I love this quote in Marjorie Hinckley's book "Small and Simple Things."

My mother taught me some basic philosophies of rearing children. One is that you have to trust them. I tried hard never to say "no" if I could possibly say "yes." I think that worked well because it gave my children the feeling that I trusted them and they were responsible to do the best they could.

I've tried to implement this advice as much as possible in my children's lives. I say yes as often as possible and even change my mind to a "yes" sometimes after saying "no." My kids are always thrilled. Like this April day in 2007 at Seuss Landing in Florida. Sage asked if she could run through the fountains at "One Fish, Two Fish, Red Fish, Blue Fish." I immediately said "no." It was a little chilly, plus I knew it would ruin her hair for future photos that day. Then I started thinking "why does it matter if she gets wet?" It's going to get warmer during the day, I have a jacket for her, and who cares if she doesn't look perfect in the photos?"

The photo at the left below tells it all. Sage was elated when I said "Yes!"

dare to live

YES by Lisa Bearnson

#50 I LOVE HOME

Why: To recall the places you've called home, to remember warm memories of what home means to you.

What do you love best about your home? How have you made it a cozy place to live? Write about some of the different places you've lived in over the years. Which place felt most like home to you and why?

bring it home

HOME by Suzy Plantamura

"Mid PLEASURES and palaces though we may ROAM, Be it ever so HUMBLE, there's no place LIKE home." —JOHN HOWARD PAYNE

MY PANTRY

Crazy, I know, but my favorite place in my house is my pantry. No—it's not because I love to eat (although I do!). My pantry represents warmth, friendship and acceptance. My kids and their friends know they never have to ask me for food. I have an "open pantry policy" and they can eat whatever they want. It does my heart good to see a neighborhood friend searching through the pantry. He or she always says "Hi Lisa" then goes back to the digging. Because of this policy, our house is always filled with lots of people. This brings lots of love, laughter and chaos. I love it because I'd rather have my kids and their friends in my home than anywhere else.

The Key to my Happy Place

share your "happy place"

MY PANTRY by Lisa Bearnson

share the love

HOMESPUN KINDNESS by Jaime Lynne Lea Woodmansee

12 JOURNALING IDEAS ABOUT HOME

1. Describe your SMALLEST home.

2. DESCRIBE your largest home.

3. Write about the HOME you loved best and the REASONS why.

4. What does "there's no place LIKE HOME" mean to you?

5. WHEN you walk into YOUR home, how do you FEEL?

6. What ITEMS in your home MAKE it feel like yours?

7. If you could change ANYTHING about your home, WHAT would it be?

8. Do you BELIEVE "home is where the HEART is"?

9. What's your favorite ROOM in your home?

10. DESCRIBE your childhood home, your PARENTS' HOME, your grandparents' HOME.

11. If YOU were going to redecorate your HOME, where would you shop for new furnishings?

12. What little TOUCHES make your house a home?

SUPPLIES

#1 Talents and Gifts

PG 6   **SHE TAUGHT ME** by Lisa Bearnson. **Supplies** *Patterned paper and jewels:* My Mind's Eye; *Felt ribbon:* Queen & Co.; *Letter stickers:* American Crafts; *Font:* Georgia, Microsoft.

PG 7   **TAKE NOTE** by Laura Kurz. **Supplies** *Cardstock:* Bazzill Basics Paper; *Chipboard letters:* Making Memories; *Stamps:* FontWerks; *Fonts:* Times New Roman and Arial, Microsoft.

PG 8   **GRANDMA'S GIFT** by Cindy Tobey. **Supplies** *Cardstock:* Bazzill Basics Paper; *Patterned paper:* Flair Designs (sheet music), My Mind's Eye (pink floral) and Scenic Route (brown dot); *Chipboard accents:* Deluxe Designs (musical note), Fancy Pants Designs (swirls) and My Mind's Eye (tag); *Acrylic letters, decorative tape and journaling sticky notes:* Heidi Swapp for Advantus; *Paint and brads:* Making Memories; *Clear label sheet:* Avery; *Ink:* Clearsnap; *Paper clip:* KI Memories; *Rub-ons:* Hambly Studios (bird) and My Mind's Eye (hand and "Play"); *Letter stickers:* American Crafts and Making Memories; *Circle sticker:* KI Memories; *Transparent overlays:* My Mind's Eye; *Font:* Goudy Old Style, Microsoft; *Other:* Thread, staples and fiber.

#2 Words to Live By

PG 10   **WORDS TO LIVE BY** by Deena Wuest. **Supplies** *Software:* Adobe Photoshop Elements 4.0, Adobe Systems; *Digital crossword puzzle:* MYO Crossword Puzzle Brush Set by Anna Aspnes, www.designerdigitals.com; *Fonts:* Garamond Pro, Adobe Systems; Avant Garde, www.myfonts.com; Gregor Miller's Friends, www.dafont.com.

PG 11   **MY GRANDPA K** by Jamie Harper. **Supplies** *Patterned paper:* Autumn Leaves; *Letter stickers and phrases:* K&Company; *Monogram letter:* Making Memories.

PG 12   **TRUTH** by Lisa Bearnson. **Supplies** *Patterned paper and jewel brads:* Imaginisce; *Chipboard letters:* Kit of the Month, Lisa Bearnson; *Paint:* Making Memories; *Pen:* Slick Writer, American Crafts.

#3 The Perfect Adventure

PG 14   **STARS IN HER EYES** by Francine Clouden. **Supplies** *Cardstock:* Bazzill Basics Paper; *Patterned paper:* Scenic Route; *Acrylic swirls and stars:* Queen & Co.; *Transparency frames:* Hambly Studios; *Acetate and chipboard letters:* Heidi Swapp for Advantus; *Letter stickers:* EK Success and Making Memories; *Journaling card, scroll stamp and label stickers:* 7gypsies; *Paint:* Crea and Raphael; *Clear adhesive:* Ranger Industries; *Pen:* Zig Writer, EK Success; *Other:* Thread.

PG 15   **SUMMER ESCAPE** by Summer Fullerton. **Supplies** *Cardstock:* Bazzill Basics Paper; *Patterned paper:* My Mind's Eye; *Tag:* Making Memories; *Glitter brads:* Doodlebug Design; *Felt letters:* American Crafts; *Stamps:* Inque Boutique; *Embossing ink:* Top Boss, Clearsnap; *Clear embossing powder:* Jo-Ann Stores; *Fonts:* FG Maria, www.fontgarden.com; Executive, Internet.

PG 15   **WILLIAMSBURG** by Candice Stringham. **Supplies** *Cardstock:* Bazzill Basics Paper; *Rub-on:* American Crafts; *Stamps:* Autumn Leaves; *Other:* Ribbon and ink.

#4 You Can

PG 16   **ATTRIBUTE** by Hera Frei. **Supplies** *Patterned paper and epoxy sticker:* Stemma; *Felt flowers:* AccuCut; *Brads:* SEI (black) and Creative Imaginations (teal and orange); *Chipboard letters:* Heidi Swapp for Advantus; *Stamps:* Rhonna Farrer; *Ink:* Brilliance, Tsukineko; *Font:* Thong, Microsoft.

PG 17   **THERE'S A GIRL IN THE HOUSE** by Terri Davenport. **Supplies** *Software:* Adobe Photoshop CS2, Adobe Systems; *Digital accent:* Beautiful Me Kit by Mindy Terasawa, www.designerdigitals.com; *Digital accent:* Labeled Female Brush Set by Anna Aspnes, www.designerdigitals.com; *Digital accent:* Home Sweet Home Brushes-n-Stamps by Katie Pertiet, www.designerdigitals.com; *Fonts:* Avant Garde BK BT, Adobe Systems; SP You've Got Mail, www.scrapsupply.com.

PG 18   **PROFESSIONAL BOUQUET CATCHER** by Susan Opel. **Supplies** *Cardstock:* Bazzill Basics Paper and Prima; *Patterned paper and "Fabulous" sticker:* K&Company; *Flowers:* Prima; *Chipboard letter:* Scenic Route; *Ribbon:* C.M. Offray & Son; *Fonts:* Rockwell (journaling and "Professional") and Rage Italic (The Bouquet" and "Catcher"), Microsoft; Triforce ("Catching"), www.dafont.com; Separates (green swirly dingbat), www.dafont.com.

#5 It's a Balancing Act

PG 20   **GOOD, BETTER, BEST** by Lisa Bearnson. **Supplies** *Patterned paper:* My Mind's Eye; *Vinyl letters and pen:* American Crafts; *Chalk:* Pebbles Inc.; *Flowers:* Heidi Swapp for Advantus.

PG 21   **DAILY DOSE** by Amanda Probst. **Supplies** *Cardstock:* Prism Papers; *Patterned paper:* American Crafts and Collage Press; *Letter tiles:* Provo Craft; *Spiral punch:* Stampin' Up!; *Corner rounder:* EK Success; *Glaze:* Glossy Accents, Ranger Industries; *Fonts:* Century Gothic, Microsoft; CK Chemistry, www.scrapnfonts.com.

PG 22   **BALANCING** by Lisa Brown. **Supplies** *Letter stickers:* American Crafts; *Pen:* Zig Writer, EK Success; *Font:* 2Peas Cross Eyed, www.twopeasinabucket.com; *Other:* Patterned paper.

#6 You're Beautiful

PG 24   **LOOKING IN** by Deena Wuest. **Supplies** *Software:* Adobe Photoshop Elements 4.0, Adobe Systems; *Digital patterned paper:* Purely Happy Paper Pack by Katie Pertiet; *Digital circles:* Graphic Pop Circles Brushes-n-Stamps by Katie Pertiet; *Digital frames:* Window Frames by Katie Pertiet, all from www.designerdigitals.com; *Digital accent:* Basic Masking Gradient Brush Set by Anna Aspnes, www.designerdigitals.com; *Fonts:* Interstate Light, www.myfonts.com; Impact, www.fonts.com.